HISTORY OF JAPANESE MARTIAL ARTS

Written by

Shihan Allen Woodman

SIDEKICK PUBLICATIONS

History of Japanese Martial Arts is published by SIDE**KICK** Publications. All written,

Photographed and/or illustrated material, in whole or in part herein is the sole property of SIDE**KICK**Publications and Allen Woodman.

All rights reserved under the International and Pan American Copyright Conventions.

SIDE**KICK** Publications is solely responsible for the printing, layout and formatting of this material.

Distribution of this text and material herein, including but not limited to text, photographs and /or illustrations by photopay or copy in whole or in part without prior written consent of SIDE**KICK** Publications is strictlyforbidden and prohibited by international law.

History of Japanese Martial Arts Written *by Allen Woodman*

1st printing Copyright– 2011 Printed in Japan 2011

2nd Printing 2014

History of Japanese Martial Arts
Written by Allen Woodman

Dedication

I thank all those who have supported and nourished the martial arts around the world.

History of Japanese Martial Arts
Written by Allen Woodman

About the cover

Designed by Allen Woodman

Photography Allen Woodman

History of Japanese Martial Arts
Written by Allen Woodman

Table of Contents

About the Author		Page	6
Chapter 1	The art of our fathers	Page	15
	Aikido	Page	23
	Judo	Page	37
	Jujitsu	Page	47
	Karate Do	Page	67
	Shotokan	Page	81
	Goju Ryu	Page	115
	Kyokushin	Page	132
	Wado Ryu	Page	142
Chapter 2	Ranking & Kyu	Page	153
Chapter 3	Looking for Our selves	Page	169

ABOUT THE AUTHOR

SHIHAN
ALLEN WOODMAN

When I first began my training at the age of four, I had no thought of the length of time that I would continue my training. My father was enlisted in the military and we moved quite often. One day the order came to pack our belongings once more as we were heading overseas for the next duty station. My family and I had to move to Japan that year. I was not there too long before I was offered an amazing chance to train in karate. I was offered to attend a karate class with my next door neighbor. I went, excited to see those kicks,

History of Japanese Martial Arts
Written by Allen Woodman

punches and throws I had seen on television with my father early on Saturday afternoons.

My first class was a much needed break from daily life on a military base with little to do and for me to get excersice as well as a way for my parents to get me out of the house for a couple hours a week. Before long it had filled my life attending classes several times a week and hours at a time. I hadn't understood the validity or the opportunity I was given at the time however; it's the basis of all my martial arts today.

I began my training with a true martial arts legend Shihan Ryuichi Sato. Sensei Sato was a long time student of the founder of traditional Japanese karate do Osensei Gichin Funakoshi. A direct student of Funakoshi Sensei but was ultimately pushed out during the takeover of the Hombu dojo in Tokyo by the newly commissioned Japan Karate Association (J.K.A.) in the late 1950's. Because of the

History of Japanese Martial Arts
Written by Allen Woodman

politics involved with the organization after Osensei Funakoshi's death in 1957, Sensei Sato decidedly stepped away and stayed away from the inner workings and union of the Hombu dojo and began his own school outside Atsugi, Japan. This is where I started my training. At age four, I didn't know that it would lead me to a lifetime of study and learning. After forty years I am still learning more about myself and my art through my training and my association with my karate family.

Training in Japan with Sensei Sato

History of Japanese Martial Arts
Written by Allen Woodman

I left Japan at age fourteen but returned several times to test for promotions and train with my sensei back in Japan. Those days were the most memorable for me as I was a grown adult with a Dan ranking. I could comprehend more and understand in a better light what karate and its inner techniques meant. The fundamentals of karate do are a never ending supply of information. To understand the basic movements and kihon of karate will develop into the more advanced stages of Karate. The understanding of karate is the fundamental foundation to all that a good karate ka will ever learn in a lifetime.

In 1988 I was received the sad news that Sensei Sato had died in Japan. It was a sever loss to me as well as many other students. The Dojo outside Atsugi, Japan would be closed and that I was to receive my 4th degree Black Belt from him posthumously, as well as the title Renshi (Master Instructor).

History of Japanese Martial Arts
Written by Allen Woodman

Sensei Allen testing for 3rd Dan at the Atsugi Dojo in 1986

In 1988 I was welcomed in to the training hall of a well respected instructor of Shotokan karate, Sensei Walter Todd. Todd Sensei was also a direct student of OSensei Funakoshi in Japan just after World War Two. In 1946 when the American occupying forces lifted the ban for martial arts training in Japan, Todd Sensei began training at the Hombu Dojo in Tokyo, Japan. Sensei Walter Todd later was granted his 5th Dan certificate directly from Funakoshi Sensei in 1956.

History of Japanese Martial Arts
Written by Allen Woodman

Sensei Walter Todd & Allen Woodman at the Dojo in Oakland, Ca.

Sensei Todd receiving his Ni Dan Certificate in Tokyo, Japan 1947

It was fantastic training and a time of learning for me to be able to study under such a great teacher as Todd Sensei. He was a wealth of knowledge and unencumbered skill. I would later receive my 3th Dan under his

History of Japanese Martial Arts
Written by Allen Woodman

direct tutelage in 1991 in the arts of Aikido and Wado Ryu.

1998 I returned to Japan full time. I settled down, lived and worked in and around Tokyo for the next fourteen years. I returned to my training but due to location and time I enrolled in the Hombu Dojo in Tokyo, Japan. It was a blessing to train with many students from around the world and learn from some of the most noted teachers available. I am proud and happy to have had that opportunity to do so.

In January, 2011, I was promoted to 6th degree black belt and continued my title of Renshi or master instructor. Soon after, there was a world altering event in Japan that would once again change my life. A catastrophic tsunami and earthquake shook the country of Japan. Thus my return to the United States was inevitable. I toured throughout the United States upon my return and began teaching seminars and informative lectures to willing participants. I recently settled down and am now living, working and teaching in lower Pennsylvania. I was offered a great job opportunity with the Central Bucks County YMCA as the Coordinator for the martial arts programming for the YMCA in Doylestown, Pennsylvania beginning in 2012. I happily accepted and am now working toward other personal goals in my martial arts career.

Since my leave from the YMCA position I have returned once again to what I know best. Teachign martial arts has always been my passion and a responsibility that I willingly accept. Travelling the world to sharre my knowledge and skills with others is a dream come true and one that I hold in the highest regard.

CHAPTER 1

THE ART OF THE FATHERS

This is History of Japanese Martial arts. This book has been put together over years of training and years of research. Inside these pages is information that will enlighten a few and reinforce the knowledge of others.

The stories contained in this material are not my personal beliefs or my opinions of these arts. They are with the best of foundations the authentic and hopefully

History of Japanese Martial Arts
Written by Allen Woodman

accurate accounts of martial arts from the students, schools and teachers of their respective arts.

With very due diligence I have talked, interviewed and researched these subjects over a 40 year period. It is not my in my interest to deny some parts of their history or origins to make some arts look better. In particularly not to make them look better than another martial arts practice either.

While my foremost study has been in the traditional Japanese karate systems, I have had extensive training outside my comfort zone. Travelling and training in arts in China, Hong Kong, Thailand, and Philippine Islands and all over the United States. I have delved deep in to the roots and foundations of some arts in this book to find the arts true origins and in some cases why they began and by whom.

It is my personal belief that the people responsible for beginning an art form must be given credit. Without their dedication and true leadership we would all be lesser martial artist ourselves.

History of Japanese Martial Arts
Written by Allen Woodman

The select few individuals in this text are only a handful of peoplethat have dedicated their entire lives to the preservation and the practice of their arts. They must also be praised for the benefit to mankind as a whole. Because of their sacrifices we have the opportunities to learn the most ancient of art forms today.

That to me is the true essence of a real martial art. Any art that has lasted through years of turmoil, hidden practices and or political refuge is an authenticated art foprm as far as Iam concerned.

As you will read forward you will find that often art forms were disallowed by governments and even outlawed by political means.

Some arts have been lost due to these issues, yet others still remain and are vibrant and active arts practiced around the world.

While researching this book I have come across finer aspects of the arts in question that may or may not be taught at other locations.It is with these fine points that I point out that it really is not the art you learn but the learning of the art that is more the meaning of martial arts.

Martial art is the study of military tactics, of defense and attack in various forms. Less we forget that the second word of this is ART. With that is the ideal that these systems have a science and nuance that is undefined by specific rules of military engagement!

They are the search for self in an altruistic manner. It is quit amusing to note that although martial arts are the techniques of defense and attack,hit, punch, kick, throw. Every art form I have come in contact with in my travels and learning all have the same basic philosophy of non aggression toward others.

Some arts make it their path to learn a peaceful way without confrontation and others accept the confrontation as a mere obstacle to peace.

Oddly, in comparison the arts that most practice will never use these martial techniques for anything other than development of self through practice and exercise.

When you think of the concept yourself, you can imagine that learning how to punch someone as a way to learn to never punch someone is a very strange approach to self-defense. Most arts have this same simple ideology however. The act of aggression is not promoted and often not tolerated. I have seen personally students have been kicked out of schools for bad destructive behavior and at point karate tournaments; I personally have disqualified students for excessive contact or unsportsmanlike conduct. The pure concept of martial arts is a peaceful serene life filled with-out conflict and with-out the use of the art they train years to master.

Ideology aside, I believe this to be a valid approach to conflict in most cases. To avoid conflict in yourself and others is the extreme ideal of a martial arts practitioner.

"It is what I strive for in my daily life and training".

History of Japanese Martial Arts
Written by Allen Woodman

Looking back, it is hard to imagine when martial arts were not a part of my life. I realize that I started training at a younger age than most people. I am positive that it reflects now in my actions and decisions for my life. It effects how I relate to others on a day to day basis, make choices in stressful conditions as well holding back on wanting to strangle the idiots who cut me off on the freeway. But patience is a virtue or it can be a waste of time.

It all depends on your perspective of the given situation."

It is much like choosing a martial art and a martial arts training school appropriate for you. It all depends on your perspective.

"All martial arts are not the same".

Martial arts come from many different countries and many different cultures. They are all born from the sole instinctive purposes of defense. Martial arts literally means in translation Military Warfare. It is the ability and skill to attack and defend.

History of Japanese Martial Arts
Written by Allen Woodman

The difference between each individual art or another is the dynamics of its use and the techniques that it incorporates.

Before I begin, I wish to stress a fundamental point. There is no style, system or art form that is greater than another. All arts are equal in their entirety. Some arts may punch and others may not. Some kick while others throw their opponent. Each style, system or art form stresses a different viewpoint, idea or perspective. The end result of all real martial arts is the same, *self-defense*. Being able to ward off an attack from various angles with pre-trained re-actions is the ultimate and ending objective of all true martial arts. Different arts have their own different history, philosophy and techniques. That is what makes them different and that is what makes them good.

It is my personal view that there is no art or style that can state it was the first. It would only be the shear arrogance and ego of man to believe that one specific style or form was the beginning of all others. As long as man has existed on this small planet, he has needed and developed the skills to defend his/her home, family, property and life against invading predators of all kinds.

I will start in alphabetical order to disregard any potential arguments or misunderstandings later on as to which one is best or first. I would not care to even begin a convoluted discussion of who thinks what culture or race was the forward to any other. It is a pointless argument that has no value or true meaning to the history or development of martial arts. These are not the only martial arts available. These are just a few select arts that I have trained in or have personal firsthand knowledge of.

Not to mention they are some of my favorites.

History of Japanese Martial Arts
Written by Allen Woodman

AIKIDO

History of Japanese Martial Arts

Written by Allen Woodman

Aikido; is a Japanese art form that originated from the ancient Japanese art of Jujitsu. Founded by the great Osensei Morihei Ueyashiba.

In the early part of 1910 Ueyashiba Sensei already had earned a sixth degree black belt in traditional Daito-ryu Jujitsu. He had once served in the Japanese (Jeitai) Army as an officer and soldier. Later in life, after the death of his father he became a devoted

Shintoist. A true Shintoist is above all else a pacifist. The story, or more legend has it that one day while taking a shower, Ueashiba Sensei shook the water from his body by a single movement. This movement is said to be his time of enlightenment. Osensei Morihei became one with his universe and understood it principles of balance and movement.

Whether you personally believe this concept is true or not is up to your personal beliefs and of your understanding of the universe around you. The late Great O'Sensei Ueyashiba probably is the closest thing I have ever heard of.

Aikido was introduced as the only true passive martial art in the world. By using attackers own force against them-selves. The Aiki practitioner maintains his center (Ki) and blends or harmonizes with his opponents' attacks and movements. This is the only passive martial art known to have ever been developed. The translation of AI KI DO is harmonizing your mind and body with the universal spirit of energy (Ki)

History of Japanese Martial Arts
Written by Allen Woodman

Osensei Morihei Ueshiba 1883-1969

This is the true nature and spirit of Aikido. It is a deeplyspiritual artform that relies on its truly passive nature. On the other hand however Aikido is the culmination, study and strategy of leverage and balance. Aikido practice is rigid in its training style.Learning to fall (Sutemi) and roll (Ukemi) is its own art form and takes years to master.

Aikido technique uses small and large circular movements to avoid, counter and maneuver an opponent off balance. This art creates great dynamic throws and sweeping turning techniques to disable, disarm and even lock an aggressor in to submission.

History of Japanese Martial Arts
Written by Allen Woodman

This art form is passive in its intent; however do not mistake its true nature for the ability to inflict severe damage to an oncoming attacker.

The founder of Aikido, Master Ueshiba Morihei, was born on December 14, 1883. Living in the turbulent time of Japan's modernization, he dedicated himself to establishing a martial art that would meet the needs of contemporary people but would not be an anachronism. The following factors were at the core of Master Ueshiba's primary concerns: an abiding love for traditional martial arts, the care that it not be misunderstood and a deep wish to revive the spiritual quality of budo.

He sought to achieve his goal through a relentless quest, given substance by constant training in the martial arts, for the truth of budo throughout the vicissitudes of modern Japanese history.

Ultimately, Master Ueshiba concluded that the true spirit of budo is not to be found in a competitive and combative atmosphere where brute strength dominates and victory at any cost is the paramount objective.

He reasoned that it is to be realized. It is the quest for perfection as a human being, both in mind and body, through cumulative training and practice with kindred spirits in the martial arts. For him only such a true manifestations of budo can have a raison d'être in the modern world, and when that quality exists, it lies beyond any particular culture or age.

His goal, deeply religious in nature, is summarized in a single statement:

"The unification of the fundamental creative principle, ki, permeating the universe, and the individual ki, inseparable from breath-power, of each person".

Through constant training of mind and body, the individual ki harmonizes with the individual ki, and this unity appears in the dynamic, flowing movement of ki-power which is free and fluid, indestructible and invincible. This is the essence of Japanese martial arts as embodied in aikido.

History of Japanese Martial Arts
Written by Allen Woodman

After Ueshiba left Hokkaidō in 1919, he met and was profoundly influenced by Onisaburo Deguchi, the spiritual leader of the Omoto kyo religion (a neo-Shinto movement) in Ayabe. One of the primary features of Ōmoto-kyō is its emphasis on the attainment of utopia during one's life. This was agreat influence on Ueshiba's martial arts philosophy of extending love and compassion especially to those who seek to harm others. Aikido demonstrates this philosophy in its emphasis on mastering martial arts so that one may receive an attack and harmlessly redirect it. In an ideal resolution, not only is the receiver unharmed, but so is the attacker.

In addition to the effect on his spiritual growth, the connection with Deguchi gave Ueshiba entry to elite political and military circles as a martial artist. As a result of this exposure, he was able to attract not only financial backing but also gifted students. Several of these students would found their own styles of aikido.

Aikido was first brought to the rest of the world in 1951 by Minoru Mochizuki with a visit to

France where he introduced aikido techniques to judo students.

Onisaburo Deguchi

He was followed by Tadashi Abe in 1952 who came as the official Hombu representative, remaining in France for seven years. Kenji Tomiki toured with a delegation of various martial arts through fifteen continental states of the United States in 1953. Later in that year, Koichi Tohei was sent by Aikikai Hombu to Hawaii, for a full year, where he set up several dojos. This was followed up by several further visits and is considered the formal introduction of aikido to the United States. The United Kingdom followed in 1955; Italy in 1964; Germany and Australia in 1965.. Today there are aikido dojos available throughout the world.

The biggest Aikido organization is the Aikikai Foundation which remains under the control of the Ueshiba family. However, aikido has many styles, mostly formed by Morihei Ueshiba's major students.

The earliest independent styles to emerge were Yoseikan Aikido, begun by Minoru Mochizuki in 1931, Yoshinkan Aikido founded by Gozo Shioda in 1955, and Shodokan Aikido, founded by Kenji Tomiki in 1967.The emergence of these styles pre-dated Ueshiba's death and did not cause any major upheavals when they were formalized. Shodokan Aikido, however, was controversial, since it introduced a unique rule-based competition that some felt was contrary to the spirit of aikido. This concept was not within the founder of Aikido's ideology of the advancement of the art. Osensei Ueashiba did not feel that competition could benefit the Aiki practitioners' universal center and understanding. It was never an accepted system of Aikido practice.

After Ueshiba's death in 1969, two more major styles emerged. Significant controversy arose with the departure of the Aikikai Hombu Dojo's chief instructor Koichi Tohei, in 1974. Tohei left as a result of a disagreement with the son of the founder, Kisshomaru Ueshiba , who at that time headed the Aikikai Foundation. The disagreement was over the proper role of *ki* development in regular aikido training. After Tohei left, he formed his own style, called Shin Shin Toitsu Aikido, and the organization which governs it, the Ki Society (*Ki no Kenkyūkai*).

A final major style evolved from Ueshiba's retirement in Iwama, Ibaraki, and the teaching methodology of long term student Morihiro Saito. It is unofficially referred to as the "Iwama style", and at one point a number of its followers formed a loose network of schools they called Iwama Ryu. Although Iwama style practitioners remained part of the Aikikai until Saito's death in 2002, followers of Saito subsequently split into two groups; one remaining with the Aikikai and the other forming the independent organization the Shinshin Aikishuren Kai, in 2004 around Saito's son Hitohiro Saito.

Today, the major styles of aikido are each run by a separate governing organization, have their own headquarters (*honbu dōjō*) in Japan, and have an international breadth.

In aikido, as in virtually all Japanese martial arts, there are both physical and mental aspects of training. The physical training in aikido is diverse, covering bothgeneral physical fitness and conditioning, as well as specific techniques.Because a substantial portion of any aikido curriculum consists of throws, the first thing most students learn is how to safely fall or roll. The specific techniques for attack include both strikes and grabs; the techniques for defense consist of throws and pins. After basic techniques are learned, students study freestyle defense against multiple opponents, and in certain styles, techniques with weapons.

Physical training goals pursued in conjunction with aikido include controlled relaxation, flexibility, and endurance, with less emphasis on strength training. In aikido, pushing or extending movements are much more common than pulling or contracting movements. This distinction can be applied to general fitness goals for the aikido practitioner.

Certain anaerobic fitness activities, such as weight training, emphasize contracting movements. In aikido, specific muscles or muscle groups are not isolated and worked to improve tone, mass, and power

Aikido-related training emphasizes the use of coordinated whole-body movement and balance similar to yoga or Pilates. For example, many dojos begin each class with warm-up exercises (*junbi taisō*), which may include stretching and break falls.

History of Japanese Martial Arts
Written by Allen Woodman

Aikido training is based primarily on two partners practicing pre-arranged forms (*kata*) rather than freestyle practice. The basic pattern is for the receiver of the technique (*uke*) to initiate an attack against the person who applies the technique—the *tori*, or *shite*, (depending on aikido style) also referred to as *nage* (when applying a throwing technique), who neutralises this attack with an aikido technique.

Both halves of the technique, that of *uke* and that of *nage*, are considered essential to Aikido training. Both are the Aikido principles of blending and adaptating. *Nage* learns to blend with and control attacking energy, while *uke* learns to become calm and flexible.

In the disadvantageous, off-balance positions in which *nage* places them. This "receiving" of the technique is called *ukemi*. *Uke* continuously seeks to regain balance and cover vulnerabilities (an exposed side), while *nage* uses position and timing to keep *uke* off-balance and vulnerable. In more advanced training, *uke* will sometimes apply reversal techniques (*kaeshi-waza*) to regain balance and pin or throw *nage*.

Unlike other arts that take a heavy toll on a person's physical well being in later years, Osensei Ueshiba was still actively teaching at the main (Hombu) school until his death in 1969. He was 81.

The Hombu Dojo for Aikido is still very active today. The head instructor of the school is the Doushou who happens to be the Grandson of Ueshiba Osensei.

History of Japanese Martial Arts
Written by Allen Woodman

JUDO

History of Japanese Martial Arts
Written by Allen Woodman

Judo; The founder of Judo, Jigoro Kano was born in 1860, he graduated with a degree in literature from Tokyo Imperial University in 1881 and took a further degree in philosophy the following year. Apart from being the founder of judo, Kano was a leading educationalist and a prominent figure in the Japanese Olympic movement.

When Kano began his study of ju-jutsu as a young man, the ju-jutsu masters of the martial arts were struggling to earn a living.

History of Japanese Martial Arts
Written by Allen Woodman

Although they were willing to teach the skills handed down to them over many generations, there was little interest among people of the succeeding generation Inaddition, the demise of the samurai (warrior) class had reduced the need for instruction. People of the new western idealogical lifestyle soon gave way to the traditions of the past. Those past customs included such martial training and / or a need to protect oneself or family in a new legal society of law and order.

At the age of 18 Kano studied the ju-jutsu of the Tenshin Shinyo Ryu under the great masters Fukudo and Iso, both instructors were the highly prestigious Komu Sho. Following the death of Fukuda, Kano remained briefly with master Iso before finishing his study with master Ikubo.

By 1883, Kano had clarified his analysis of ju-jutsu and related methods to the point at which he felt able to instruct the public through a school of his own. To that end he borrowed a small room at Eishoji temple and opened the first school which he called the Kodokan for the study of Kano judo.

Judo although a new art was not initself new. It was a culmination of not only the traditional Jujitsu practice of Osensei Kanos youth but also his professorship study of physiology, body movement and human engineering that led him to the creation of this new art of Judo.

Professor Jigoro Kano 1860-1938

Judo is an art that derives its birth from the traditional Japanese art of Jujitsu. It was the sole theory of Professor Jigaro Kano of the Imperial University in Tokyo, Japan around

History of Japanese Martial Arts
Written by Allen Woodman

the turn of the last century. In approximately 1898 when the first paper was published on Ju-Do By Dr. Kano, He was an attending sixth degree black belt of Jujutsu at the main training school (Hombu Dojo). At the same time he was the head professor at the Tokyo University in the field of anatomical theory and physiology.

It is the study and research of the body's movement and muscular bio-structure. In short he was a true master of understanding the body and how it moves.

Ju-Do or the supple way in its translation, is the practice of leverage and off-balancing your advisory with throws and locking movements. By using a push and pull (Suri-Komi) method to throw and pin an attacker it relies a great deal on balance and strength training to hone the principles that it so greatly uses with such effortless grace.

With-in the first ten years of its initial conception the style of Judo became a national sport in Japan.

History of Japanese Martial Arts
Written by Allen Woodman

The country at this time was already geared up to increase its push into the foreign lands of China and Korea. Looking for a true Japanese art, the politico of Japans monarchy decided to introduce the new system in to the mainstream populace as the national sport. A move designed to heighten the moral of the Japanese public and mobilizing troops for the intellectual premise of supposed superiority.

Originally, Judo had in its make-up three forms (Katas) as well as striking (Tsukiwaza) techniques. However, since its main inception in to the 1956 Olympics, the art of Judo discontinued the practice and training of strikes, kicks and punches as well as its original three forms. There are few people left alive today that remember or have ever been taught the original katas of Judo.

When the first dojo of Judo had opened in 1883, a number of machi dojo (backstreet gyms) decided that the Kodokan was conceited and ought to be put in its place. They visited its premises and caused damage so that if honor were to be satisfied a challenge match

History of Japanese Martial Arts
Written by Allen Woodman

Prof. Jigaro Kano demonstrating his Judo

would have to be arranged. At such matches the Kodokan was represented by Sakujiro Yokoyama, the outstanding player of his day, and the result was invariably a win for Kano judo.

History of Japanese Martial Arts
Written by Allen Woodman

To gain acceptance from the provinces Kodokan representatives travelled all over Japan giving lectures and demonstrations on the principles behind the new method. The finale of these lectures was a contest, with limb locks and striking excluded, between the Kodokan lecturer and a member of the local training school.

A particularly important match took place in 1886 to decide which system of ju-jutsu should be approved for use in military academies, police departments and public schools. The 15 strong male Kodokan team defeated all opponents and judo became a government approved sport.

The aftermath of the 2nd World War was a dark era for Japan and all things Japanese. As part of Japan's war effort, instructors had been ordered to teach unarmed combat. After the end of World War II with occupational forces in the land and governing over the newly recovered country, and in retaliation the occupation forces prohibited almost all practice of the martial arts in schools and public institutions. The ban remained in place until 1951.

In 1949, however the occupation authorities indicated that the yudanshakai (dan grade society) of the various private schools and training halls could be reconstituted as a single democratic organization.

As a result the Japanese Judo Federation was formed under the presidency of Risei Kano, only son of Jigoro Kano, with headquarters at the Kodokan. Today the All

Japan Judo Federation has Jigoro Kano's grandson as its President.

Although there had been a gradual relaxation of the rule during allied forces occupation, private instruction in judo was tolerated and the police were exempted from the general prohibition. The Kodokan was largely left to re-establish itself unhindered.

Kano had taken a stand against the worst aspects of militarism in pre-war Japan and that, together with new draft rules which removed the vestiges of judo's martial origin and made Kodokan Judo practice and training acceptable to the authorities.

Whatever political backing might have done to push it to the outward world, it is an art form that commands respect as a practical and applicable martial art and highly effective method of self-defense.

History of Japanese Martial Arts
Written by Allen Woodman

JUJITSU

History of Japanese Martial Arts
Written by Allen Woodman

Jujitsu; formally known as Jiujitsu-do. Also seen spelled as Jiujitsu, Jujutso, Jiujutsu, and Jijitsu, Jujitsu is one Japan's oldest martial arts. Through the ages it has been known by many different names, such as "yawara," "taijutsu," "wajutsu," "torite," "kogusoku," "kempo," "hakuda," "kumiuchi," "shubaku," and 'koshinomawari."

The word Jujitsu means "gentle art" ("ju" means flexibility or gentleness and "jitsu" means art or technique). Jujitsu is a system of combat where a smaller person may defeat a much larger person by adding the larger person's strength and momentum to the application of his or her own technique.

Although it is considered the "gentle art," Jujitsu is not a delicate art. It was the primary unarmed combat method of the samurai and could be devastatingly brutal when used on the battlefield. Westerners tend to misinterpret "gentle" to mean weak or the use of little strength or power.

This was never the case with combat Jujitsu where great strength was frequently needed to defeat an enemy. Not all Jujitsu techniques are gentle, though sometimes they are done with such swiftness and efficiency that they appear to be so. Therefore, gentleness is more correctly interpreted as flexibility, where the mind and body unite and flow with the power and motion of an opponent to defeat the opponent. Sometimes this results in great force being used.

Most Jujitsu techniques cause great pain and some may break bones with little effort. This is especially noticeable when applying techniques to pressure points where minimum effort may cause maximum pain. Using pressure points allows you to make someone move where you want him or her to go, or you can use them to cause enough pain to make your opponent surrender.

The term "gentle art" really refers to the principles and techniques that are the foundation of the art. In Jujitsu, you learn not to resist. When pushed, you pull. When pulled, you push. This is the principle of "Ju no ri."

History of Japanese Martial Arts
Written by Allen Woodman

Jujitsu's origin is lost in the mists of antiquity. Some say it originated in China around the 7th century BC, while others say it originated in Japan. In either case, the Japanese perfected the art.

Legend has it that Jujitsu was originally introduced to Japan by a Chinese named Chen Yuan-ping, in the mid 1600's, but a large amount of evidence disproves this. For instance, there are reliable records of the Japanese Jujitsu masters, such as Hitotsubashi-Joken or Sekigushi-Jushin, who thrived years before this date. Authentic descriptions of Jujitsu are found in documents such as Yukisenjo-Monogatari, Kuyamigusa, and in old Jujitsu "Densho," the instructions and records of secrets by the founders of various Jujitsu schools, which also predate the legend.

Many factors led to the development of Jujitsu. Carrying bladed weapons was common during ancient times and successful unarmed defense against them was a great asset. The Japanese soldier was trained from a young boy to be skilled with many weapons, like the Japanese katana, a two-handed, razor-sharp sword. They also trained with the halberd, javelin, combat-scythe, bow and arrows, and other smallerweapons. Since warriors of the time wore armor, kicks and punches had little effect, so chokes and joint locks were used to attack unprotected areas, such as the neck, arms, and legs.

Other factors are: Before the advent of firearms in Japan, bows and arrows were used in warfare, but in close combat, warriors used spears and swords. Occasionally, they had to fight with their bare hands using (Kumiuchi). The more advanced techniques of Kumiuchi contributed to the development of Jujitsu For centuries,

Japanese warriors wore two swords, one long and one short. However, warriors in the presence of high personages had to appear without long swords.

History of Japanese Martial Arts
Written by Allen Woodman

Jujutsu is the Martial Art invented by the Samurai.

In the Tokugawa period, long swords were taboo in the court of the Shogun, while the retinu on guard and minor officials were allowed to wear short swords. These warriors and guards, as well as prison guards, needed a way to defend themselves without resorting to the deadly sword. Special methods, such as punching, poking, chopping, kicking, and bending and twisting the joints, were studied

History of Japanese Martial Arts
Written by Allen Woodman

and developed so that an unarmed person, or a person who was restrained from using his weapons, could subdue an adversary.

For several hundred years before the Meiji era, and throughout the feudal age, class distinction was rigidly enforced between the warrior and the commoner, the latter being forbidden to wear any sword. So, for self-defense, commoners had to learn the art of bare-handed fighting. The afore mentioned factors are closely interlocked and cannot be clearly separated from one another.

For a historical study of Jujitsu there are two main sources: (1) historical and literary works in general, and (2) the various Densho.

History books contain comparatively few references to Jujutsu, but there are more to be found in the miscellaneous writings of each period. As for the Densho, each school, in their eagerness to enhance their school prestige, they often adorned their origins and records with flowery rhetoric, so some times their contents are not reliable. Moreover, some Densho, while of ancient origin, are actually

History of Japanese Martial Arts
Written by Allen Woodman

manuscript copies so their authenticity is dubbious. Nevertheless, it may be safely deduced from the records available that Jujutsu began to take a systematized form in the latter half of the 16th century and that the various schools came into being from the 17th to about the beginning of the 19th centuries.

The Nihon Shoki, "The Chronicle of Japan," a history compiled by the Imperial command in 720 AD, refers to a tournament of "Chikara- Kurabe", a contest of strength, which was held in the 7th year of the Emperor Suinin, 230 BC.

Some historians regard this as the beginning of Sumo (Japanese wrestling) which has some aspects in common with Jujutsu. Although it is questionable whether Chikara-Kurabe bore any relation either the Sumo or Jujitsu of later years, the recorded event is historical proof of their embryonic stage.

The first instance of the word "yawara" occurring in Japanese literature is found in the Konjaku-Monogatari, the Once-upon-a-time Stories, which are said to have been written during the latter half of the 11th century. Since the word is found in a story about Sumo, it cannot be directly linked to Jujutsu, but it deserves the attention of Jujutsu historians.

Jujutsu's tenets (doctrinal principles), the instructions of the various schools mostly dwell on the ideas which may be seen in the famous old book on strategy selected by the Chinese strategist, Hwang-Shihkon, which was the Bible of warriors in the feudal age. They also carry echoes of Chinese philosophy represented in the Book of Lao-tsze, who preached non-resistance and gentleness, or in the Yi-King (or I Ching), the Book of Changes. There is little original thinking in the school writings, although occasionally one encounters passages which indicate an aspiration to the ideal of Bushido.

Around 1100 AD, Shinra Suburo Yoshimitsu created Daito ryu-Aiki-Ju-Jutsu, which involved techniques where a small person may control a bigger, more powerful person with soft, simple movements. This was a new concept to the Japanese, since powerful techniques were the norm. Since Yoshimitsu

History of Japanese Martial Arts
Written by Allen Woodman

was a General for the Minamoto family, his Jujutsu was kept a secret inside that family for centuries. Through the centuries, the public gradually gained knowledge of its techniques.

From 1333 to 1573, Jujutsu was popular in Japan and many styles, or "ryus," developed. More than 700 styles were officially accounted for in Japan during the 17th century. The first Ryu opened in 1532 by the Japanese Takenouchi Hisamori. His system, based on combat Sumo-wrestling techniques, gave Jujitsu an identity.

Some styles involved weapons, while others were purely unarmed. When Shogun Tokugawa rose to power around 1600, commoners were forbidden to carry weapons, so unarmed self-defense was popular among them.

Jujutsu was very popular with the samurai since empty hand fighting was common in battle. Also, if a lesser samurai ever had to subdue a higher ranked samurai, he could do it using Jujitsu with impunity. Whereas, if he used a sword, which could result in a death of either of the samurai, the Lord would be angered and might seek punishment for the lesser samurai.

Some claim Takenouchi Ryu was the core ryu (school) from which all Jujutsu ryus sprang. This ryu was founded in 1532 and borrowed substantially from Sumo. Takenouchi Ryu adapted combat methods from various sources that came to be known as "Kogusoku." This method and others were later classified under the common heading of Jujutsu.

One problem with Jujutsu was that it was so violent that was difficult to practice. Tournaments usually ended with serious injuries and even death. However, this was also a time when new techniques were developed since people could fight to the death.

Gradually, wars decreased in number and peace became more common. During these times, Jujutsu developed into a more of a weaponless martial art, although schools taught both armed and unarmed combat. Some schools were based either hard or soft techniques, some focused on kicking and punching, some focused on throwing, and yet others focused on joint-locks and takedowns.

According to the Bujutsu-Ryusoroku, the Biographies of the Founders of Various Martial Exercise Schools, in the 1800's some twenty schools of Jujutsu (ryu) existed, such as the "Takenouchi Ryu," "Sekiguchi Ryu," "Kyushin Ryu," "Kito Ryu," "Tenshin-Shinyo Ry," " Tenjin-ryu," and "Daito-ryu."

The differences between these various schools were chiefly attributable to specialization in certain techniques, but it seemed that a few Jujitsu masters merely founded new schools simply for their own purposes, for there were schools that differed in name but were practically identical in substance.

Two main styles of Jujitsu were developed, Ju-jutsu and Aiki-Jutsu. Unlike Ju-Jutsu, Aiki-Jutsu was kept secret. Only a few people were taught this art, Jujutsu has spawned a number of martial arts, including Judo, Aikido and possibly Korean Hapkido and Kuk-sool. In 1882, Jigoro Kano, who had studied Kito Ryu and Tenshin-Shinyo Ryu, founded Kodokan Judo (gentle way). Morihei Uyeshiba was one of the few Aiki-Jutsu students and he used what he learned to develop Aikido (way of universal power) in 1898.

In 1871, the Decree Abolishing the Wearing of Swords, which forbid samurai from wearing swords in public, was devastating for all martial arts. People no longer needed to know how to defend themselves from armed enemies since swords were now prohibited in public, so martial art school attendance dropped rapidly. It was a difficult time for all martial art schools.

In 1886, the Japanese police department was looking for a martial art to teach all their employees. They arranged a competition between the Jujutsu school and the Judo school. The ferocity of jujutsu became its downfall. Kano had removed most of the extremely violent moves from Jujutsu when he developed Judo so it could be practiced without the risk of seriously hurting people. The Judo students were better athletes and defeated all but two of the Jujutsu students. Those two matches ended in a tie. Therefore, the Japanese police choose Judo. However, they later reinstated most of the Jujutsu strikes because they were needed. This new art became known as "Taiho Jutsu," which was only taught to the police and military. After this competition, Judo was recognized as the better art and Jujutsu was left to fend for itself.

Beginning in the early 1900's, Japanese Jujutsu masters began visiting the United States and Europe exhibiting their skills and techniques. In the 1930's, Jujutsu began to grow and be recognized in the United States.

Jujutsu has evolved into an art that is much safer to practice today than it was in the time of the samurai.

Modern Jujutsu is not a contest of muscular strength, nor does it attempt to maim or kill. It uses throws, locks, kicks, and punches to gain release from an attacker and to temporarily incapacitate him or her. It is applicable to women and men of all ages and sizes. It places priority on practicing self-defense, while adhering to local laws relating to self-defense.

One large strength of Jujutsu is that you can learn and choose techniques to use without concern about competition rules and their limitations. It covers the entire spectrum of different realistic types of attacks, including kicks, punches, knees, elbows, throws, take-downs, joint-locks, ground-fighting and more.

Jujutsu is an excellent form of exercise, especially when considering the importance of maintaining or increasing one's flexibility, endurance, and strength, and is also good practice for children. It builds up self-confidence, co-ordination, and it teaches them respect, discipline and other social benefits. Although Jujutsu is categorized mostly as a system of self-defense, competitions, especially in Brazilian Jujutsu (as popularized by the Gracie family), have become more common.

Jujutsu theory is derived from the way techniques are applied. Each technique is applied to cause pain compliance (thus the term weeping) before moving into another technique. This means the defender must use proper form in the technique for it to be painful to the attacker. It also helps attacking students develop pain tolerance.

Some of types of techniques found in modern Jujutsu are: Atemi-Waza (striking techniques) Nage-Waza (throwing techniques) Kensetsu-Waza (joint manipulation) Shime-Waza (strangulation or choking techniques) Katami-Waza (ground techniques), Vital and nerve point striking and manipulation

History of Japanese Martial Arts
Written by Allen Woodman

This art goes back farther than its own records do. Before the feudal period of Japans notorious history, the leading family (Diamyo) of traditional Jujutsu was said to be the family of Takenouchi.

The Takenouchi house was a ruling family of the Japanese period around the year 345 A.D. The Takenouchi clan taught and trained imperial troops (Teino-No-Keibi) or Samurai and Warlord militia (Shogun-no Bushi) for several hundred years.

The most popular and better known style of Jujutsu however, was the Daito Ryu system taught by the Daito family house (Diamyo), popular around the year 465 A.D.

The many different styles and systems of Jujutsu uses leverage, locking and throwing techniques to disable, strike and even kill an assailant. There is very little kicking involved in this art. If any kicks are delivered they are low and direct only. This art is often associated with grappling and ground fighting practice as its basic techniques are taught from a kneeling or siting position.

History of Japanese Martial Arts
Written by Allen Woodman

The basic reason for developing most of these lower grounded techniques are because of the position of the sword carrying warriors that practiced the art. Most guards and warriors sat in a kneeling position (Seiza) while in the presence of their commander. Bent on their knees with their feet crossed slightly at the toes and tucked under the weight of their body and armor they might be wearing. So any defense would first need to be learned from that sitting position.

From this father art there came a multitude of other off shoots and singular arts such as Aikido and Judo. Their foundations are solidly with in the practice of traditional Jujitsu but have in some way moved away from the original principles of Jujutsu to form their own identity.

Goshin, HakkoRyu, Taizan Ryu, Small Circle and many others have over time been developed through traditional training in formal Jujutsu

Some arts have denied or lost their connection with the parent art but if you research the history of most grappling arts you would surely find the traditional art of Jujutsu to be somewhere in its history.

History of Japanese Martial Arts
Written by Allen Woodman

KARATE-DO

History of Japanese Martial Arts
Written by Allen Woodman

Karate; is the Japanese art of self-defense created by the basic principles and roots of Chinese Kung Fu. This art draws its fundamental tools of use from power and balance. Karate is a direct, linear martial art utilizing force and focus to disable and defend against any would be attacker.

History of Japanese Martial Arts
Written by Allen Woodman

Actual Karate history can be traced back some 1400 years, to Daruma, founder of Zen Buddhism in Western India. Daruma is said to have introduced Buddhism into China, incorporating spiritual and physical teaching methods that were so demanding that many of his disciples would drop in exhaustion. In order to give them greater strength and endurance, he developed a more progressive training system, which he recorded in a book, Ekkin-Kyo, which can be considered the first book on karate of all time.

The physical training, heavily imbued with Daruma's philosophical principles, was taught in the Shaolin Temple in the year 500 A.D. Shaolin (Shorin) kung-fu, from northern China, was characterized by very colorful, rapid, and dynamic movements; the Shokei school of southern China was known for more powerful and sober techniques. These two kinds of styles found their way to Okinawa, and had their influence on Okinawa's own original fighting method, called Okinawa-te (Okinawan hand) or simply te. A ban on weapons in Okinawa for two long periods in its history is also partly responsible for the high degree of development of unarmed fighting techniques on the island.

In summary, karate in Okinawa developed from the synthesis of two fighting techniques. The first one, used by the inhabitants of Okinawa, was very simple but terribly effective and, above all, very close to reality since it was used throughout many centuries in real combat. The second one, much more elaborate and impregnated with philosophical teachings, was a product of the ancient culture of

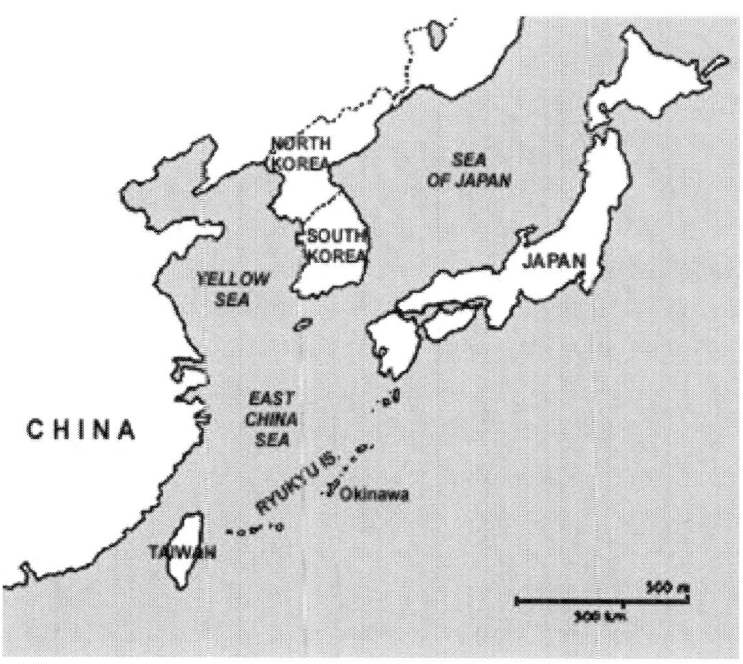

History of Japanese Martial Arts
Written by Allen Woodman

China. These two origins explain the double character of Karate--extremely violent and efficient but at the same time a strict and austere discipline and philosophy with a nonviolent emphasis.

Karate today is popularly known as a Japanese martial art of unarmed combat utilizing dynamic strikes and kicks to subdue an aggressive opponent. The mixed origins of this art however lie - geographically - much further away than mainland Japan, through the island of Okinawa in the Ryukyu island chain and ultimately to the south-east area of China in the Fujian province (Fukien). Time and circumstance have also played important roles in the formulation and development of the art, with influence from Japanese martial arts stretching back to the Heian period. To cap it all off, both the armed and unarmed arts were tested and made practical on the battlefield over several centuries of inter-tribal warfare.

All of these influences - and more - have fathered the birth of karateOkinawa was militarized long before the advent of recorded history and localized war was as common there as anywhere else where competing tribes fought to protect themselves. Mainstream Japanese fighting techniques and philosophies entered the island from the Heian period (794-1185) onwards through visiting aristocrats whobrought with them a retinue of bodyguards that were skilled in the use of the halberd, spear and sword, and who could perform archery (the chosen art of the samurai before the sword gained ascendancy) and grappling.

This knowledge was absorbed by indigenous warriors exposed to it and put to good use in violent territorial disputes among local warrior chieftains between the seventh and fifteenth centuries. One such example cited by Patrick McCarthy (though it is disputed by some historians) was the influence of Minamoto Tametomo of the Minamoto clan. According to McCarthy, in his career Tametomo overran Kyushu (the southernmost area of mainland Japan) after being exiled to Oshima Island (in the Izu Island chain) following defeat by the Taira clan and his subsequent escape. From Kyushu, Tametomo moved further south to Okinawa. Marrying into the family of a local warlord Tametomo's son, Shunten, went on to

History of Japanese Martial Arts
Written by Allen Woodman

become the most powerful warrior chief on the island with his dynasty lasting until 1253, a period in which martial arts from the Japanese mainland became further embedded into the Okinawan way of fighting. This is the story believed by certain residents in Okinawa, but historians argue the events are fictitious and were created at a later date to attempt to legitimize Japanese dominion over the Ryukyu Islands.

MinamotoTametomo was famed for his skill with the bow, the 'badge' of the samurai class before the katana and wakizashi emerged as the more famous signifiers of the warrior elite.For the next two centuries localized warfare continued between three primary areas until, in 1429, Sho Hashi was able to emerge victorious and form a centralized government.

Though 1429 is a significant date in the overall history of Okinawa, a date of more importance to the history of karate is 1507 when Sho Shin-O ratified the 'Act of Eleven Distinctions', one of which prohibited the ownership and stockpiling of private weapons. Suddenly there was no access to weapons as a

History of Japanese Martial Arts
Written by Allen Woodman

means of personal self-defense and, at a deeper level, the techniques and martial strategies that had developed under the influence of the armed warriors from mainland Japan had no apparent means of expression. Without a physical sword the technique and strategy of using a blade in combat appear to become redundant. From 1507 onwards then the people of Okinawa turned to the investigation of unarmed combat techniques in lieu of the possibility of making an armed response to an aggressor. These weaponless fighting approaches would, many changes later, one day become various schools of karate.

As important is the date of 1507. It is in important date the historical development of karate, It was the year that the Governing body made the ban on the ownership of weapons in Japan and its outlaying island territories.

The earliest recorded contact between Okinawa and China occurred in the early 7th century. Commerce and cultural exchange were slow to develop though and it was not until 1372, shortly after the demise of Mongol dominance in China, that an envoy was sent from China to Okinawa to invite the latter to become a tributary. Under the terms of the alliance trade between the two nations would increase and by the close of the 14th century a Chinese trading mission (known as the 'Thirty-Six Families') had been established in the capital city Naha. For the next five centuries, until the Ryukyu Islands were annexed by Japan in the 1870s, Chinese language and culture, including martial arts, was disseminated through Okinawa and the island chain. Close relations between the two countries also led to outstanding young Okinawan scholars being given the opportunity to travel to China to further their studies, opening the door for Chinese martial arts to be learned at the source and then transmitted back to the island.

One class within feudal Okinawan society that did perpetuate the practice of Chinese-influenced combative arts was the Pechin. The Pechin were middle-ranking warriors, somewhat equivalent to mainland Japanese samurai. Like the other classes, the Pechin were created by Sho Shin and served in an official capacity from 1509 to 1879. Unlike the higher ranking classes, the Pechin occupied positions and conducted affairs that brought them into direct contact with lower ranking citizens. For example, the Pechin could be employed in civil administration or law enforcement. It was members of the Pechin class pursuing a career in maintaining a lawful peace who can take more credit that any others for sustaining the practice of unarmed combat under direct Japanese authority.

The Shimazu clanwere firmly entrenched in the Satsuma peninsula approximating modern-day Kagoshima prefecture in the extreme southern area of Kyushu Island.

The clan was famous for their strong sword style of Jigen ryu. They were suffering after failed campaigns in Korea under Toyotomi Hideyoshi and after defeat at the Battle of Sekigahara in 1600, the final great battle that led to the establishment of the Tokugawa Shogunate. With a high number of samurai retainers and little in the way of spoils of war to repay them Shimazu Yoshihisa, the leader of the Shimazu clan, turned his eyes southwards. The Shogunate was only too happy to bleed the

Shimazu further and distract them from any thoughts of rebellion. Thus, in 1609, an invasion fleet set sail and swept down the Ryukyuan island chain defeating all opposition as it went and occupying the islands taken.

Victory was swift. The Shimazu samurai were battle-hardened and there was little the Okinawans could do, moreso given that significant portions of the populace had had no access to weapons for 100 years. After three months of fighting Shuri castle was captured and the Shimazu took control of Okinawan political affairs. One result of this was the strict enforcement of a weapons ban, thereby finalizing the policy initially set forth by Sho Shin-O almost one hundred years earlier.

Jigen ryu is the battlefield sword art of the Satsuma samurai. As peace was established throughout the Ryukyu Islands select Pechin traveled to Satsuma peninsula and received training in this art. One such person was "Bushi" Matsumura, an important figure in the historical development of karate. Matsumura synthesized indigenous Okinawan fighting techniques with those of China arts and Jigen ryu. Notable among his students were Itosu Anko and Asato Anko, two men that would play a later crucial role in formalizing and popularizing Shuri te, while also heavily influencing Funakoshi Gichin, a man who would go on to do more than anyone to spread karate around Japan and beyond.

Another interesting historical development occurred much earlier when the second generation headmaster of the Jigen ryu, Togo Bizen no Kami Shigekata, was ordered by the head of the Shimazu clan to teach some rudimentary fighting skills to the farming population of Okinawa in case of an invasion; the peasant population could operate as a militia. This influence has been recorded in a folk dance known as the Jigen ryu Bon Odori.

Finally, it was also under Shimazu rule that kobudo developed. Kobudo is the combative use of common everyday implements such as the eiku (boat oar), the Kama (sickle) and the famous nunchaku (rice flail).

Contrary to popular belief then, Shuri te (the forerunner of the Shotokan style created by

Funakoshi Gichin and which spawned offshoots such as Wado ryu, Kyokushinkai and Shotokai) was not a simple amalgam of Chinese martial arts and Okinawan te.

This is in contrast to the Naha te style introduced to Okinawa by Kanryo Higaonna which was most definitely a Chinese martial art (most likely some kind of Crane school) modified to a certain degree on Okinawa but free from the influence of the Jigen ryu. The Shimazu invasion and subsequent exposure to Jigen ryu that some masters had was a vital event in the development of what has become modern day karate do.

Shimazu control of Okinawa ended in 1868 with the Meiji Isshin (the restoration or revolution) that put the Emperor back in control of Japan curtailing the rule of the Tokugawa shogunate). This event signaled the beginning of the modernization of Japan. Within just a few decades Japan went from a non-industrialized economy with little to no modern acccutrements to be on the world stage. Industry changed radically along with the political scene; the army and navy were modernized ending the age of the samurai once and for all.

History of Japanese Martial Arts
Written by Allen Woodman

SHOTOKAN KARATE DO

History of Japanese Martial Arts
Written by Allen Woodman

Shotokan karate; with the simultaneous eradication of the samurai class and their warrior ethos and the rise of a modern army trained to use the latest weaponry Japan's traditional martial arts suddenly found themselves irrelevant. The modern army was made up of conscripts who by necessity had to be trained as quickly and efficiently as possible. There was no impetus to developing a warrior

History of Japanese Martial Arts
Written by Allen Woodman

from birth. Further, the traditional martial arts - both armed and unarmed - were clearly unable to compare to the devastating effectiveness of rifles and artillery. Not only did it take less time to train a soldier to use a firearm, that firearm was infinitely more efficacious. The traditional fighting arts were set to decline.

The days of the samurai were over.Against this backdrop of modernization the classic arts (bujutsu) reinvented themselves as predominantly a way of life (budo). Kenjutsu became kendo, or the way of the sword, while ju jutsu became judo, or the soft way. While retaining a core of combative techniques, the emphasis was less on practical application in a fight and more on developing the morality of practitioners while fostering a sense of 'Japanese Cultural and tradition.' in the face of Westernization.

Japan's Monbusho (Ministry of Education) wholeheartedly supported the spread of various budo in the school system and so the (modified) techniques of yesteryear reached a new and wider audience. Training was serious and a sense of shugyo (austerity in practice) prevailed.

In its drive towards modernization and in pursuit of a foreign policy that would win it colonial possessions similar to those of the main European powers, Japan introduced a draft requiring male Japanese citizens to serve for a period of time in the military in 1873. This draft now included the Okinawans. While undergoing mandatory medical testing two men in particular stood out as exemplary specimens of fitness: Hanashiro Chomo and Yabu Kenetsu. After some investigation it was discovered by the military authorities that these men enjoyed a superior physique and level of endurance through their practice of karate.

Despite positive first impressions though, the Japanese military finally abandoned the idea of introducing karate as a discipline for recruits owing to the apparent lack of organization, impractical training methods and the time commitment needed to develop sufficiently. While not officially endorsed by the military then, karate was from this period taught in schools, possibly with the ulterior motive of conditioning teenagers to be able to better serve their country when drafted, but at the very least to be more productive in Japanese society.

The ultimate goal of the Empire was Asian domination and control. For this the Japanese Empire would need much in the way of a trained and skilled warrior class that would be deadly and efficient in its ability to dispatch an enemy with little to no effort.

The famous karate master Itosu Anko led this movement along with other notable characters in the evolution of karate. A trade-off was required that would have a lasting impact on the development of the art: for karate to become more widespread and popular the emphasis in training had to be changed. Removing hard core self-defense applications in lieu of teaching children, a new generation of masters introduced the group practice of kata to promote physical well-being. The original bunkai, or combative applications of the kata movements were all but lost until the close of the 20th century when the 'secrets' began to be shown and taught once again in conjunction with kata.

History of Japanese Martial Arts
Written by Allen Woodman

A sketched portrait of Anko Itosu

Itosu Anko was a defining force in the formulation of modern day karate. He created and taught the Pinan kata; simplified patterns of movement derived from the longer and more complex traditional kata. These kata were later changed by Funakoshi Gichin to become the Heian kata. Both the Pinan and Heian kata are still taught today and are among the first kata students from around the world will study and learn.

Itosu was a well-educated man and worked as a scribe to Shotai, the last king of the Ryu Kyu islands, until the monarchy was dissolved in 1879.

In 1901, Itosu placed Karate onto the physical education program of the Shuri Jinjo elementary school. As it stood Itsou believed Karate to be too dangerous to be taught to children and set about disguising the more dangerous techniques contained within the katas. As a result of these modifications, the children were taught the katas as mostly blocking & punching. This enabled the children to gain benefits such as improved health and discipline from their karate practice without giving them knowledge of the highly effective & dangerous fighting techniques that the katas contain.

History of Japanese Martial Arts
Written by Allen Woodman

In 1905, Itosu was appointed as karate teacher to the Prefectural Dai Ichi Collage and the Prefectural teachers' training collage. In 1908 Itsou wrote a letter to the Prefectural education department that outlined his views on karate and asked that karate be introduced onto the curriculum of all Okinawan schools. Itsou was granted his wish and karate became part of the education of all Okinawan children. Itsou died in 1915, aged 85.

Itosu was a great formulator & developer of Kata and it is said that he learned the kata 'Chaing-Nan' from a Chinese martial artist who was living in the Tomari region. It was this kata that provided the basis for the Pinan series. Itsou remodelled and simplified Chaing-Nan into the five Pinan Katas. The Pinans also include fighting techniques from other katas present in the Shuri region at that time. It is said that Itosu changed the katas name from Chaing-Nan to Pinan as he found 'Chaing' too difficult to pronounce. The Pinan katas are often thought of as training methods for beginners or children and are hence undervalued by more experienced karateka. The main reason for the katas being viewed this way is the fact that they were first established at the time Itsou was introducing Karate to the Okinawan schools.

Pinans Katas were developed over a period of time and were meant for to be a synthesis of the best methods being practised in the Shuri region. When karate was introduced to the Okinawan schools the Pinans would be the natural choice because they are relatively short.

The main difference between the adults and children's training would simply be a matter of approach, as opposed to any change in subject matter. As mentioned earlier, the children would be taught the katas as 'block and punch' whereas the adults would receive instruction in all the methods contained within the katas including striking to vital points, throws, chokes, strangles, joint locks, hair pulling, gouging methods etc. One of the problems with karate today is that it is the children's applications that are most commonly practised. This has lead to the majority of karateka practising the art as a rather limited striking system as opposed to

History of Japanese Martial Arts
Written by Allen Woodman

the complete fighting system it was intended to be of the four major Japanese styles of karate (Shotokan, Wado-Ryu, Goju-Ryu, & Shito-Ryu) practised throughout the world today only Goju-Ryu does not practice the Pinan / Heian Katas.

The reason the Pinan katas are common to the three remaining styles is that Itsou features strongly their family trees. Master Itsou along with Kanryo Higaonna were the main teachers of Kenwa Mabuni (founder of Shito-Ryu). The name 'Shito' is derived from the two characters used in the writing of 'Itosu' & 'Higaonna'. Mabuni was undoubtedly Itosu's foremost disciple. Along with Master Azato & Master Matsumura, Itosu was also one of the teachers of Gichin Funakoshi (founder of Shotokan). It is doubtful that Funakoshi learnt the Pinans directly from Itosu as Funakoshi concluded his training with Itsou before the Pinans came into being. Some sources say that Funakoshi learnt the Pinan katas from Kenwa Mabuni in 1919, four years after Itosu's death. Kenwa Mabuni, Gichin Funakoshi & Choki Motobu (who also studied under Itosu) were the main karate teachers of Hironori Otsuka (founder of Wado-Ryu). Otsuka also studied Shinto Yoshin Ryu jujitsu under Yukiyoshi Tatasusaburo Nakayama. Otsuka received his instruction in the Pinan katas from both Mabuni and Funakoshi.

The word 'Pinan' means, 'peaceful mind.' The name is taken to mean that once these five forms and their applications have been mastered the karateka can be confident in their ability to defend themselves in most situations. The word 'Pinan' is made up two ideograms. The original Okinawan pronunciation of the first ideogram is 'pi', whereas the Japanese pronounce it 'hei.' Generally Wado-Ryu & Shito-Ryu favour the Okinawan pronunciation of 'Pinan'.

Shotokan stylists favour the Japanese pronunciation of 'Heian.' The reason for this is that Gichin Funakoshi gave all the katas practised within Shotokan Japanese names. He did this so that the Japanese people would find the names easier to use, to further distance the art from any of its Chinese origins and to acknowledge the development of karate by the Okinawans & Japanese. Gichin Funakoshi also swapped the 'Nidan' (2nd level) & 'Shodan' (1st level) suffixes so that the names reflected the order in which the katas are most commonly taught. This means that Shotokan's 'Heian Shodan' is called "Pinan Nidan" in the remaining styles and vice-versa.

There are differences in the ways that the various styles perform the Pinan / Heian katas but the overall pattern remains the same. These changes are the result of the developments made by the founders of each style. There are also minor variations between many of the instructors and associations that are in existence today. There is nothing automatically wrong with these variations. Variations due to forgetfulness, insufficient study, poor technique, laziness etc. are obviously undesirable but this does not mean that all variations are unacceptable. Every one of us is different and hence it is impossible for everybody to perform the katas in exactly the same way. Subtle changes over time are, to my mind, actually desirable as it is in this way that karate continues to evolve.

History of Japanese Martial Arts
Written by Allen Woodman

Japan of course already had a rich history of martial arts and, as noted before, the traditional arts of kenjutsu and jujutsu had both already morphed into kendo and judo respectively. These arts were organized and well represented. To become popularly accepted karate would have to emulate these arts.

This move towards a level of standardization acceptable to the Butokukai (the National governing body for Japanese martial arts) saw many changes including the establishment of a training uniform (the gi), the use of a standardized curriculum and the use of kyu and dan gradings to reflect a student's progress within that curriculum, and the introduction of a sporting element. One of the biggest changes though was the name itself.Dai Nippon Butoku Kai, China Hand Becomes Empty Hand

Owing itself to the increasing level of nationalism in Japan in the 1920s and 1930s especially China and Chinese people in general were denigrated. Originally karate was made up of two ideograms. The second (te) was and would remain read as 'hand'. The first ideogram

History of Japanese Martial Arts
Written by Allen Woodman

though (pronounced 'toude' or 'kara') referred to China's Tang dynasty and was taken to mean 'China'. Karate (or toudi depending on who was speaking) meant 'China Hand'.

The official district records, however, show that his birth took place in 1870, but he in fact later stated he falsified his own records in order to be able to take the Tokyo Medical School entrance examination. In spite of passing the exam Funakoshi sensei never did become a member of the medical profession. Something millions of karate students around the world, myself included, will always be very grateful for his initial learning and eventual teachings of what is now known as karate

The main focus of Karate is to strike swiftly and effectively. Simplicity is a prominent virtue of traditional Karate. "One punch, one kill" It is the motto deemed by serious karate practitioners.

The most interesting aspect of Karate is its history. It seems to have basically started with China and Japan. The Chinese government had been trying to take control over the close islands of Okinawa and the Japans for several hundred years prior. The Chinese attempt to own the Japans well documented throughout history, going as far back as 1192 A.D. When the Mongolian ruler Genghis Khan built an armada of ships and set sail for the Japan islands from the Korean province. The attempt failed by an uncalculated typhoon in the Sea of Japan. The mighty ruler Khan tried again in 1229 A.D. and yet again the attacking armed ships were destroyed by yet another sudden typhoon. The surviving few ships and armies were swiftly conquered when they reached the Japan shore. The Japanese banded together and defeated easily the remaining few. Feeling the gods had favored them, not once but twice against the attacking Chinese neighbors they dubbed the storms the Kamikaze (Divine Wind).

Since then china had pursued a more political route to the same end. The island of Okinawa is in the center between the main island of Japan (Honshu) and the mainland of China. In the mid- 1800`s China had begun setting up several small communities to

History of Japanese Martial Arts
Written by Allen Woodman

influence the native Japanese owned territory. The intention was to show how much greater the Chinese way of life was and accumulate the island slowly through business and commerce.

What does this have to do with Karate? You might ask. Well, another facet of this scheme was to show a formal Chinese martial art to the native inhabitants of Okinawa. It's main aim was to try and tear the proverbial fabric of honor and respect from the warrior class of the Japanese (Bushi-Do). He had demonstrated the strength and ability of the Chinese martial art over that of the traditionally taught Japanese fighting arts (Budo).

The Chinese political leaders had selected only a few families of Japanese descent and Chinese up-brining to learn in detail the basics of Chinese Hands (Tou De-Te). In 1921 the chosen head family to demonstrate this art to the public was the clan of Itosu. The duty lied in the hands of the eldest son of the Itosu family heritage. However, just before a large demonstration was to be presented in mainland Japan, Itosu's father past away and the son was honor bound to show respect and attend the funeral proceedings. The responsibility fell to the next in line of teaching succession, OSensei Gichin Funakoshi to teach the Demonstration in Kyoto, Japan, which at that time was the official center of all martial arts.

OSensei Funakoshi was from another successful Japanese born, Chinese intergrated family of Okinawa. Born in 1868, he began to study karate at the age of 11, and had been a student of the two greatest masters of the time, Azato and Itosu. He grew so proficient that he was initiated into all the major styles of karate in Okinawa at the time.

Since he was considered a frail child many members of his family felt that he was destined for a short and uneventful life. Little did his family know just how long and how important his life would really be.

It was during his early primary school years that he was first introduced to the study "Toude Te" or "Chinese Hand" under Master Yasutsune Azato, since his family felt that studying the art of karate might help to strengthen him physically and thus improve the quality of his life.

A good student Gichin Funakoshi flourished under the tutelage of Master Azato to whose home he travelled each evening to practice karate. It was not until later Master Azato would introduce him to another important teacher under whom he would also study, Master Yasutsune Itosu. It was these two men more than any others who would have the greatest impact on his life.

No longer interested in entering the medical school it was while studying karate that Gichin Funakoshi decided to become a school teacher and so after passing the qualifying examination he took charge of his first primary school class in 1888. It was a profession he was to follow for more than thirty years.

A high point in Gichin Funakoshi's karate took place on March 6, 1921 when he had the honor of (replacing Itosu Sensei) demonstrating the art of "Okinawan Te" to then Crown Prince Hirohito during a visit he made to Okinawa.

In this rush to change presenters the Chinese backers had missed one very important factor.

Rare Photo of O'Sensei Funakoshi with both Azato and Itosu Sensei

Sensei Funakoshi wrote in Japanese (Kanji) and spoke in the daily conversational Japanese language. Kanji is the formal written

History of Japanese Martial Arts
Written by Allen Woodman

Chinese language and although the basis of Japanese writing (Kanji) is derived from the Chinese characters they have been slightly altered and changed in respect as to how they are read culturally.

Japan had another form of writing also called Hiragana. This too is rooted in the Chinese form of writing but the characters are also altered for the Japanese use. On all of the displayed printing of the performance from Sensei Funakoshi, it was read by the Japanese in what they considered to be Japanese writing. Tou De-Te in Chinese kanji is read in Japanese as Kara-Te (Empty-Hands). As no weapons were used in this art form itcaught on as a new Japanese method of self-defense.

This shift in reading wasn't immediately popular in Okinawa and it was sometime later (1936 in Okinawa as opposed to 1933 in Japan) that the new reading was officially ratified.

While the ideogram 'kara' was being read in a new way karate also became officially a 'do' as in judo and kendo. 'Do' means a way or a path and carries with it, in my opinion, three meanings. First karate do should be seen as a way of life that will (second) bring the practitsioner into contact with the Universal DO

Kara	Te	Do
Empty	hands	way (or method)

(Tao or Dao in Chinese - thereby relating the art also to Taoism) at which point (third) the art becomes a means of expressing that harmony with the Universal Do. With the change in name from toudi jutsu to karate do a deeper spiritual meaning to one's training was established.

The next turning point of Karate was still come. Then, in the spring of 1922, Gichin Funakoshi traveled to Tokyo where he had been invited to present his art of Tode-Te at the First

History of Japanese Martial Arts
Written by Allen Woodman

National Athletic Exhibition in Tokyo, which had been organized by the Ministry of Education. After the demonstration he was strongly urged by several eminent groups and individuals to remain in Japan, and indeed he never did return to live in Okinawa. Influential politicians had set Sensei Funakoshi up with a school in Tokyo behind his house (Kan). Funakoshi, who was also a respected writer and poet of his time often wrote his poetry (Hyaiku) in his pen name, "Shoto", denoting the sound of the wind blowing through pines.

When students would go to learn the art (Do) of the empty hand (Karate) at Funakoshi's house (Kan), it is said much easier in Japanese. The students learned Karate Do at Shoto's Kan, which became later known throughout the world as Shotokan Karate. It was the first formally taught Japanese martial art school at the turn of the century. It was this new form of karate that was principally introduced to Japan and made popular by Funakoshi Gichin. His students, upon completion of a later new dojo, named the training room the Shoto Kan or Shoto's Hall, and thus the first Japanese style of karate was born: Shotokan karate.

History of Japanese Martial Arts
Written by Allen Woodman

The Original Dojo of Shotokan was located in Suidobashi (Suidobata), Tokyo

As it had been in Okinawa, the educational system of Japan was to become a major factor in the spread of karate. By 1924 Sensei Gichin Funakoshi had started to introduce karate to several of the local universities, first at Keio, followed by Chuo, Tokyo, and Waseda to name but a few. It was through these universities that he was able to reach a much larger audience and this single main factor contributed greatly to the growing popularity of karate in Japan and eventually the World at large.

History of Japanese Martial Arts
Written by Allen Woodman

Osensei Gichin Funakoshi   1868-1957

Father of traditional Japanese Karate Do

History of Japanese Martial Arts
Written by Allen Woodman

Master Funakoshi was finally able to establish the Shoto-kan dojo in 1936, a great landmark in the history of karate. Funakoshi sensei had combined the techniques and katas of the two major Okinawan styles to form his own style of karate, as a result, today Shotokan karate-do includes the powerful techniques of the Shorei style of karate, as well as the lighter more flexible movements of the Shorin style of karate.

For Master Funakoshi, the word "karate" eventually took on a deeper and broader meaning through the synthesis of these many methods, becoming karate-do, literally the "way of karate," or of the empty hand. Training in karate-do became an education for life itself. A long-term student of Chinese Hands, Funakoshi was now elected to travel to Tokyo and hold a lengthy seminar and demonstration of this "new" art form.

Master Funakoshi taught only one method, a total discipline, which represented a lifestyle by design. His karate was a true path to self and the surrounding environment.

History of Japanese Martial Arts
Written by Allen Woodman

Master Funakoshi Gichin was a principle architect in the modernization and popularization of karate, leads his students in group kata practice.

Following defeat in World War Two the Japanese martial arts were for a short time banned completely. Karate didn't suffer such great oppression as it could be described as (and also was

understood by the occupying forces) a form of boxing. Shorn of all militarism the first non-Japanese students began training (American servicemen) and the JKA (Japan Karate Association) was established teaching Shotokan. The JKA organized an instructor's program and eventually sent out the cream of its cadre around the world to spread the art. Sensei included such luminaries as Nishiyama Hidetaka, Asai Tetsuhiko, Kanazawa Hirokazu and Enoeda Keinosuke. Other teachers of other forms of karate followed this example and the exchange was facilitated when foreign students began traveling directly to Japan to train in the top dojo (the honbu). As these foreign students themselves became accredited teachers the art was able to spread further and nowadays you can find a formal or informal dojo in most populous areas in any first world country. Karate has quickly become a very popular form of self-defense, a sport, a method of keeping fit, an academic subject and a spiritual discipline for millions of people worldwide.

In the beginning Funakoshi sensei taught only sixteen katas, they were: Kankudai, Kankusho, five Heian katas (known in Okinawa as Pinan katas), three Tekki katas (known on Okinawa as Naihanchi katas), Wanshu, (later to be known as Empi), Chinto, (later to be known as Gankaku), Patsai, (later to be known as Bassai), Jitte, Jion, and Seisan (later to be known as Empi), since he felt that sixteen katas were more than enough for one lifetime.

The First Inscription reads Karate ni no sente nashi

"There is no first strike in karate"

The final part of the inscription reads:

Ken Zen Ichi - The fist and Zen are one

History of Japanese Martial Arts
Written by Allen Woodman

Later in life Funakoshi Gichin studied Zen at Engakuji Temple and expanded his understanding of the ideogram 'kara' (empty) and took it back to its Buddhist origins. For Funakoshi the meaning of 'kara' also embraced the Buddhist idea that there was no thing (mu - nothing) in the Universe and by extension no duality. Through Funakoshi in particular the latter reading of karate became popular and this reading has been perpetuated.

The memorial dedicated to Funakoshi Gichin rest at the temple grounds at Engakuji, Kamakura. A shrine to the founder of modern Karate was donated by family friends and students of the traditional culture and study of ZEN. The memorial sits adjacent to the ZEN practice hall. It has been cared for and visited by thousands of followers of his teachings

History of Japanese Martial Arts
Written by Allen Woodman

"The ultimate aim of karate lies not in victory nor defeat, but in the perfection of the character of its participants"

Gichin Funakoshi Sensei

History of Japanese Martial Arts
Written by Allen Woodman

Shotokan DojoKun

Read the words from the top down and from right to left.

Hitotsu. Jinkaku kansei ni tsutomuru koto

Hitotsu. Makoto no michi wo mamoru koto

Hitotsu. Doryoku no Seishin wo yashinau koto

Hitotsu. Reigi wo omonzuru koto

Hitotsu. Kekki no yu wo imashimuru koto

First. Seek perfection of character

First. Protect the way of the truth

First. Foster the spirit of effort

First. Respect the principles of etiquette and respect others

First. Guard against impetuous courage and refrain from violent behavior.

History of Japanese Martial Arts
Written by Allen Woodman

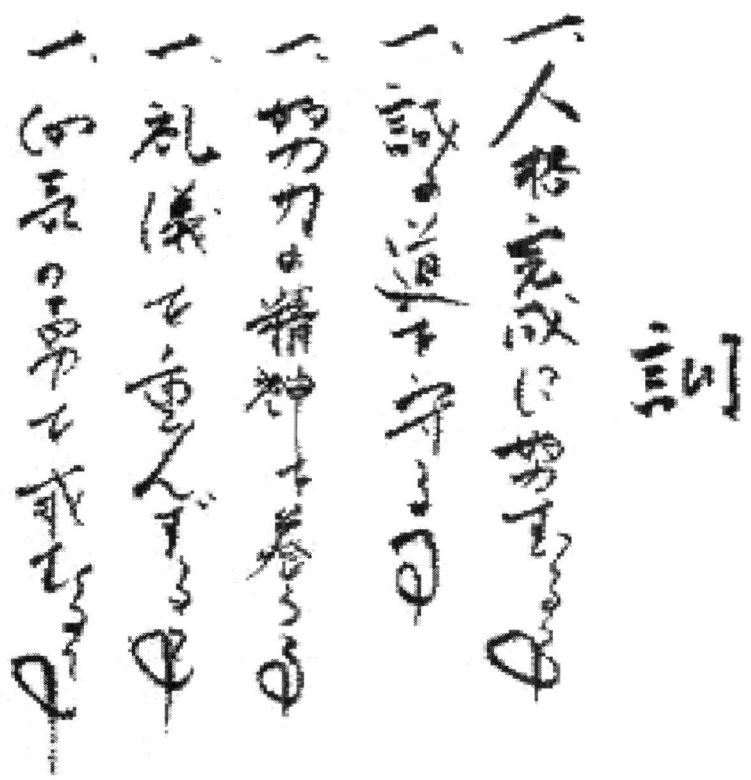

Shotokan Karate Niju Kun

The 20 precepts that are considered the rules of martial conduct written by OSensei Funakoshi

1. Karate-do begins with courtesy and ends with rei.

2. There is no first strike in karate.

3. Karate is an aid to justice.

4. First know yourself before attempting to know others.

5. Spirit first, technique second.

6. Always be ready to release your mind.

7. Accidents arise from negligence.

8. Do not think that karate training is only in the dojo.

9. It will take your entire life to learn karate, there is no limit.

10. Put your everyday living into karate and you will find "Myo" (subtle secrets).

11. Karate is like boiling water, if you do not heat it constantly, it will cool.

12. Do not think that you have to win, think

rather that you do not have to lose.

13. Victory depends on your ability to distinguish vulnerable points from invulnerable ones.

14. The out come of the battle depends on how you handle weakness and strength.

15. Think of your opponent's hands and feet as swords.

16. When you leave home, think that you have numerous opponents waiting for you.

17. Beginners must master low stance and posture, natural body positions are for the advanced.

18. Practicing a kata exactly is one thing, engaging in a real fight is another.

19. Do not forget to correctly apply: strength and weakness of power, stretching and contraction of the body, and slowness and speed of techniques.

20. Always think and devise ways to live the precepts of karate-do every day.

History of Japanese Martial Arts
Written by Allen Woodman

GOJU RYU KARATE

History of Japanese Martial Arts
Written by Allen Woodman

Gōjū-ryū; (Japanese for "hard-soft style") is one of the main traditional Okinawan styles of karate, featuring a combination of hard and soft techniques. Both principles, hard and soft, come from the famous martial arts book

Bubishi (Chinese: *wu bei ji*), used by Okinawan masters during the 19th and 20th centuries. **Go** which means hard, refers to closed hand techniques or straight linear attacks; **Ju** which means soft, refers to open hand techniques and circular movements.

Major emphasis is given to breathing correctly. Gōjū-ryū practices methods that include body strengthening and conditioning, its basic approach to fighting (distance, stickiness, power generation, etc.), and partner drills. Gōjū-ryū incorporates both circular and linear movements into its curriculum. Gōjū-ryū combines hard striking attacks such as kicks and close hand punches with softer open hand circular techniques for attacking, blocking, and controlling the opponent, including locks, grappling, takedowns and throws.

The development of Gōjū ryū goes back to Kanryo Higashionna, (1853–1916), a native of Naha, Okinawa. Master Higashionna began studying Shuri-te as a child. He was first exposed to martial arts in 1867, when he began training in Monk Fist Boxing (*Luohan*

Quan) under a master named Aragaki Tsuji Pechin Seisho, a fluent Chinese speaker and translator for the Ryukyu court. In 1870, Aragaki had to go to Beijing to translate for Okinawan officials. It was then that he recommended Higashionna to another master named Kojo Taitei, who he began training under. With the help of Taitei and a family friend, Higashionna eventually managed to set up safe passage to China, lodging, and martial arts instruction. In 1873 he left for Fuzhou in Fujian Province, China, where he began studying Chinese boxing under various teachers.

In 1877 he began to study under a kung fu master called Ryū Ryū Ko (or Liu Liu Ko, or To Ru Ko; the name is uncertain.) Tokashiki Iken has identified him as Xie Zhongxiang, founder of Whooping Crane Kung Fu. Zhongxiang taught several Okinawan students who went on to become karate legends.

Higashionna returned to Okinawa in 1882 and continued in the family business of selling firewood, while teaching a new school of martial arts, distinguished by its integration of *gō-no* (hard) and *jū-no* (soft) kempo into one system. Higashionna's style was known as Naha-te. Gojukai history considered *Chinese Nanpa Shorin- ken was* the strain of kung fu that influenced this style

Kanryo Higashionna, circa early 1900s

History of Japanese Martial Arts
Written by Allen Woodman

Higashionna's most prominent student was Chojun Miyagi (1888–1953), the son of a wealthy shop owner in Naha, who began training under Higashionna at the age of 14. Miyagi had begun his martial arts training under Ryuko Aragaki at age 11, and it was through Aragaki that he was introduced to Higashionna. Miyagi trained under Higashionna for 15 years, until Higashionna's death in 1916.

In 1915 Miyagi and a friend Gokenki went to Fuchou in search of Higashionna's teacher. They stayed for a year and studied under several masters but the old school was gone (Boxer Rebellion 1900). Shortly after their return, Higashionna died. Many of Higashionna's students continued to train with him and he introduced a kata called Tensho which he had adapted from Rokkishu of Fujian White Crane.

Higashionna's most senior student Juhatsu Kyoda formed a school he called Tōon-ryū (*Tōon* is another way of pronouncing the Chinese characters of Higashionna's name, so *Tōon-ryū* means "Higashionna's style"), preserving more of Higashionna's approach to Naha-te.

In 1929 delegates from around Japan were meeting in Kyoto for the All Japan Martial Arts Demonstration. Higashionna asked Miyagi to go as his representative; Miyagi was also unable to attend, and so he in turn asked his top student Jin'an Shinsato to go. While Shinsato was there, one of the other demonstrators asked him the name of the martial art he practiced. At this time, Miyagi had not yet named his style. Not wanting to be embarrassed, Shinsato improvised the name *hanko-ryu* ("half-hard style"). On his return to Okinawa he reported this incident to Chojun Miyagi, who decided on the name *Gōjū-ryū* ("hard soft style") as a name for his style.

Chojun Miyagi took the name from a line of the poem *Hakku Kenpo*, which roughly means: "The eight laws of the fist," and describes the eight precepts of the martial arts. This poem was part of the Bubishi, a classical Chinese text on martial arts and medicine. The line in the poem reads: *Ho wa Gōjū wa Donto su* "the way of inhaling and exhaling is hardness and softness," or "everything in the universe inhales soft and exhales hard."

In March 1934, Miyagi wrote *Karate-do Gaisetsu* ("Outline of Karete-do (Chinese-hand)"), to introduce karate-do and to provide a general explanation of its history, philosophy, and application. This handwritten monograph is one of the few written works composed by Miyagi himself.

Miyagi's house was destroyed during World War II. In 1950, several of his students began working to build a house and dojo for him in Naha, which they completed in 1951. In 1952, they came up with the idea of creating an organization to promote the growth of Goju-Ryu. This organization was called *Goju-Ryu Shinkokai* ("Association to Promote Goju-Ryu"). The founding members were Seko Higa, Keiyo Matanbashi, Jinsei Kamiya, and Genkai Nakaima.

History of Japanese Martial Arts
Written by Allen Woodman

Chojun Miyagi Sensei

There are two years that define the way Goju-ryu has been considered by the Japanese establishment: the first, 1933, is the year Gōjū-ryū was officially recognized as a budō in Japan by Dai Nippon Butoku Kai, in other words, it was recognized as a modern martial art, or gendai budō. The second year, 1998, is the year the Dai Nippon Butoku kai recognized Goju-ryu Karate do as an ancient form of martial art (*koryu*) and as a bujutsu. This recognition as a *koryu bujutsu* shows a change in how Japanese society sees the relationships between Japan, Okinawa and China. Until 1998, only martial arts practiced in mainland Japan by samurai had been accepted as *koryu bujutsu*.

In addition to his personal training and development of Naha-te, Miyagi Chojun Sensei spent a great deal of his time promoting the art. In 1921, he performed a demonstration of Naha-te in Okinawa for the visiting Prince Hirohito, Emperor of Japan, and in 1925 for Prince Chichibu. Miyagi

Chojun Sensei had already envisioned the development of Naha-te not only in Japan but also around the world. It became increasingly important to organize and unify Okinawan karate as a cultural treasure to be passed on to future generations. In 1926, Miyagi Chojun

Sensei established the Karate Research Club in Wakas-Cho.

Four instructors, Miyagi Chojun, Hanashiro, Motobu and Mabuni, taught alternately some preliminary exercises and supplemental exercises. Afterwards, Miyagi Chojun Sensei gave talks to the students about mankind, daily life, and the samurai code of ethics in order to improve their moral development as well.

In 1927, Kano Jigoro Sensei, founder of Judo, saw a demonstration of a kata by Miyagi Chojun Sensei and was impressed by the advanced technique and sophistication of Naha-te. Kano Sensei?s influence allowed Miyagi Chojun Sensei to perform Okinawan karate at leading Japanese Budo tournaments sponsored by the government. In 1930, Miyagi Chojun Sensei performed at the Butoku-kai Tournament and at the Sainei Budo Tournament in 1932.

As its exposure increased, many became interested in Miyagi Chojun Sensei's art. One of Miyagi Chojun Sense's senior disciples, Shinzato Sensei, gave a performance of kata at a Japanese martial arts tournament. Afterwards, a master asked the name of his school. Shinzato Sensei had no answer for him, returned to Okinawa and told Miyagi Chojun Sensei about his encounter. In order to promote his art as well as cooperate with other schools of Japanese martial arts, Miyagi Chojun Sensei decided it was necessary to name his art. It became known as "Goju Ryu" Karate, meaning "hard and soft" taken from the precepts of traditional Chinese Kempo (see below). He was the first among different schools of karate to name his art and in 1933 his art of Goju Ryu was formally registered at the Butoku-kai, Japanese Martial Arts Association.

During the 1930's, Miyagi Chojun Sensei actively developed and promoted karate-do in Japan and throughout the world. For example, in 1934, a Hawaiian newspaper company invited him to Hawaii in order to introduce and populate karate in Hawaii. In 1936, Miyagi Chojun Sensei spent two months in Shanghai, China, for further study of Chinese martial arts. In 1937, he was awarded a commendation by the Butoku-kai for his kata. Miyagi Chojun Sensei developed Goju Ryu by analyzing and employing scientific methods of exercise. In 1940, he created katas "Gekisai Dai ichi" and "Gekisai Dai ni" with the purpose of popularizing karate and improving the physical education of young people. He also created "Tensho" kata emphasizing the softness of the art whereas "Sanchin" kata emphasizes the hardness.

A tragic period ensued in the 1940's as a result of World War II and Miyagi Chojun Sensei stopped teaching. During this period he lost a son and a senior student while

History of Japanese Martial Arts
Written by Allen Woodman

enduring the devastations of war and poverty. After the war, Okinawan karate spread rapidly throughout mainland Japan. Miyagi Chojun Sensei taught karate in Kansai, Japan, for a short time. In 1946, however, he started teaching karate at the Okinawan Police Academy as well as in the backyard of his home in Tsuboya where his son still lives today.

From the beginning, Miyagi Chujun Sensei recognized karate as a valuable social treasure of Okinawa. He devoted his entire life to the study, development and transmission of Okinawan karate for the sake of future generations and is truly known as the founder of Goju Ryu karate-do. During his lifetime, Miyagi Chojun Sensei was known and respected by everyone not only in Okinawa but also respected throughout the world as one of karate?s greatest authorities.

Miyagi Chojun Sensei chose the name "Goju Ryu" from the "Eight Precepts" of traditional Chinese Kempo found in the document "Bubishi?" and are as follows:

History of Japanese Martial Arts
Written by Allen Woodman

1. *The mind is one with heaven and earth.*
2. *The circulatory rhythm of the body is similar to the cycle of the sun and the moon.*
3. *The way of inhaling and exhaling is hardness and softness.*
4. *Act in accordance with time and change.*
5. *Techniques will occur in the absence of conscious thought.*
6. *The feet must advance and retreat, separate and meet.*
7. *The eyes do not miss even the slightest change.*
8. *The ears listen well in all directions.*

These eight precepts are the essence of the martial arts and are the elements one strives to achieve in training Goju Ryu Karate-do. Such training shall serve to lead humankind to rediscover our natural instincts and capabilities.

One of the greatest known modern instructors of this art was the legendary and often outcasted Sensei Gogan (the Cat) Yamaguchi. A strong developed teacher of the Okinawan art of Goju Ryu he insisted on perfection of techniques from his students and

History of Japanese Martial Arts
Written by Allen Woodman

trained in the traditional ways of Goju Ryu Karate Do. Daily training methods included running and Tasio (warm up exercises)on the beach , in the mountains and the woods of Okinawa. Communing with nature was in his belief the only true path to understanding its meaning and developones mind and body at the same time.

Sensei Yamaguchi was the strongest proponent of karate and more specifically Goju Ryu system during the early 20th century .Often pictured under a large waterfall practicing his Goju Ryu breathing techniques developed by his teacher Chojun Miyagi.

Yamaguchi Sensei was one of a handful of students that had trained directly with Chojun Miyagi Sensei and followed the path of true martial artist and Goju Practitioner.

History of Japanese Martial Arts
Written by Allen Woodman

Gogan "The Cat" Yamaguchi Sensei

History of Japanese Martial Arts
Written by Allen Woodman

KYOKUSHINKAI KARATE DO

History of Japanese Martial Arts
Written by Allen Woodman

Kyokushinkai karate; was developed by Masutatsu Oyama, the founder of the largest Karate organization.It started and established a Bare-knuckle, Full-contact tournament system one of the top authoritative and influential figures in the world of Martial Arts history one of the pioneers in spreading the Asian Martial Arts to the West and to all over the world ever pursuing, ever a practitioner, he is recognized to be reached to the level of the true Mastery.

He was a kind and friendly man off the mat, but when he was on the mat he always

History of Japanese Martial Arts
Written by Allen Woodman

felt a need to prove every technique with power. I have dedicated this section to the man who has profoundly changed many peoples perspective of martial arts and training, Sensei Mas Oyama. Many people have turned rumor in to stories in to historical data and don't actually know the true facts. Sensei Masutatsu Oyama was born into the Moon family on July 12, 1923 in Korea. He lived on his sister's farm from infancy until age 12.

During the Japanese occupation of Korea he quickly integrated himself with Japanese language and customs. One way to integrate with the Japanese was to work with them or for them. He became a Japanese officer's errand boy. This was of great significance at the time because of his acceptance of the Japanese occupation he was offered to train in Japanese karate with other Japanese soldiers. As a young teen he was already a large bodied individual. He got the name Oyama from other Japanese soldiers because of his large size. O-yama means Big Mountain.

History of Japanese Martial Arts
Written by Allen Woodman

When the war escalated in China the officer whom he had helped for several years offered to adopt him and take him to Japan. Oyama travelled to Japan in 1938. Sensei Oyama enrolled in Tokushoku University in Tokyo, Japan and was accepted to train with Funakoshi Osensei for two years. He trained in various martial arts disciplines in Japan earning his second degree (Nidan) black belt in karate at age 17, and fourth degree *(yondan)* at age 20. The progress he made in his studies of Judo was equally astounding, achieving the rank of *yondan* or fourth degree black belt in less than four years. In 1947 Oyama entered and won the first Japanese martial arts Championships and won. Oyama was also known for fighting bulls by his bare hands.

On several occasions he practiced with live bulls, having the bulls charge him. As he stood his ground till the last second stepping aside to kill the charging bull with a single strike to the neck, killing the bull instantly. He often cut the bulls horns off with a single bare hand strike to horn. He fought a total of 52 bulls, killing three and breaking the horns off 49 others during the 1950s; his many fights with the bulls were documented by local press. Oyama sensei was even memorialized in a popular Japanese manga or comic book the called *Karate Baka Ichidai* (literal title:"*A Karate-Crazy Life*"). Oyamas exploits were depicted in this weekly comic and brought great fame to his Karate and to him personally.

One Teacher of Mas Oyama was So Nei Chu. He was to have a profound influence on Mas Oyama, when he advised him to make a firm commitment to dedicate his lifeto the martial way. Heeding his words to "seek solace in nature", Mas Oyama subjected himself to the rigours of daily training in the mountains of Chiba prefecture in order to strength his own body and spirit. He was accompanied by one of his own students, but after six months of isolation, the student secretly fled, leaving Mas Oyama to continue his vigourous training alone. Returning to civilization after one year of solitude, he tested his abilities in the karate division of the first national martial arts championships, and won.

Mas Oyama then imposed on himself a further period of solitary training, again in the mountains, and upon his return, demonstrated his remarkable ability by fighting bulls.

His notoriety spread rapidly as his feats were unparallel and in 1954 he opened his first dojo in Tokyo, Japan. This dojo was the beginning of the Kyokushin KaiKan. In 1964, the Tokyo Honbu (headquarters) was officially opened and theInternational Karate Organization (IKO) was established. Today, the

IKO, headed by Kancho Shokei Matsui, is the largest karate organization in the world with over twelve million members in 135 countries

His fame as a Karateka spread rapidly as his feats were unparalleled and in 1954 he opened his first dojo in Tokyo, Japan.

This dojo was the beginning of the Kyokushin KaiKan. In 1964, the Tokyo Honbu (headquarters) was officially opened and the International Karate Organization (IKO) was established. Today, the IKO, headed by Kancho Shokei Matsui, is the largest karate organization in the world with over twelve million members in 135 countries. As the Father of Kyokushinkai Karate he has spawned what is now known as K-1 fighting. These matches are sold out events worldwide.

The *kanji* (Japanese characters) calligraphy, worn universally on the front of the *gi*, simply means "Kyokushinkai", which is the name given by Sosai Mas Oyama to the karate style he created. It is composed of three characters:

Kyoku meaning "Ultimate".

Shin meaning "Truth" or "Reality".

Kai meaning "Society" or "Association".

The symbol of Kyokushin Karate is the *Kanku*, which is derived from Kanku Kata, the Sky Gazing Form. In this kata, the hands are raised and the fingers meet to form an opening through which the sky is viewed. The top and bottom points of the *Kanku* represent the first fingers of each hand touching at the top and the thumbs touching at the bottom, symbolizing the peaks or ultimate points. The thick sections at the sides represent the wrists, symbolizing power. The centercircle represents the opening between the hands through which the sky is viewed, symbolizing infinite depth. The whole *Kanku* is enclosed by a circle, symbolizing continuity and circular action.

History of Japanese Martial Arts
Written by Allen Woodman

Founder and Sosai Masutatsu Oyama
1923-1994

History of Japanese Martial Arts
Written by Allen Woodman

WADO RYU KARATE DO

History of Japanese Martial Arts
Written by Allen Woodman

Wado Ryu Karate-Do ; was founded circa 1935-40 and since its inception, it has become one of the five major styles in Japan. Its popularity is increasing worldwide, yet surprisingly, very little literature has been written about Wado Ryu. Thus, "open the window" to this little exposed style. (Wado Ryu translated means "way of peace").

Sensei Hironori Otsuka founded the system of Wado-Ryu. Sensei Otsuka was born in 1892. Otsuka's philosophy entailed to mix power, speed and subtlety. He originally studied ju-jitsu at Wasada University in Tokyo.

History of Japanese Martial Arts
Written by Allen Woodman

He received many credentials and began to study under such noted masters as Matsumura and Nakayama. It was during this time that Otsuka began training with the famous Gichin Funakoshi, thus, came the introduction of the Okinawan influence upon karate-do. It is due to Otsuka's influence that Wado Karate emphasizes smaller, more focused movements.

The name Wado-Ryu comes from the idea of TEN TO CHI TO JIN NO RI_DON RI WA SURU. The Kanji TEN means sky, heaven and the air, CHI stands for earth, the soil and the ground. JIN represents men, mankind and human beings. RI_DO means reason and truth. WA stands for the sum of a whole, peace and harmony. These definitions are the peace and harmony. These definitions are kanji's literal meanings, but imply many other concepts and symbols which encompass the existing world such as sunlight, rain harvesting crops, desire, love etc. The phrase TEN TO CHI TO JIN NO RI_DO NI WA SURU, connects all these symbols and concepts together with TEN, (sky) CHI (ground) and JIN (human beings). Represented as three circles, meaning the basic principles. If those combinations are naturally executed then WA (harmony) is created and that is represented by a larger circle that encompasses all the other principles involved in the system. Creating harmony - WA is the most difficult condition to attain in the martial arts. In order to do this you have to sharpen your intellect not only through physical training but mental training as well.

The name *Wadō-ryū* has three parts: *Wa*, *dō*, and *ryū*. *Wa* means "harmony," *dō* means "way," and *ryū* means "style." Harmony should not be interpreted as pacifism; it is simply the acknowledgment that yielding is sometimes more effective than brute strength.

From one point of view, Wadō-ryū might be considered a style of jūjutsu rather than karate. It should be noted that Ōtsuka embraced Shotokan and was a chief instructor at the Hombu dojo for a time. When Hironori Ōtsuka first registered his school with the Dai Nippon Butoku Kai in 1938, the style was called "Shinshu Wadō-ryū Karate-Jūjutsu," a name that reflects its hybrid character.

Ōtsuka was a licensed Shindō Yōshin-ryū practitioner and a student of Yōshin-ryū when he first met the Okinawan karate master Gichin Funakoshi. After having learned from Funakoshi, and after their split, with Okinawanmasters such as Kenwa Mabuni and Motobu Chōki, Ōtsuka merged Shindō Yōshin-ryū with Okinawan karate. The result of Ōtsuka's efforts is Wadō-ryū Karate rather than Wadō-ryū JuJitsu.

To the untrained observer, Wadō-ryū might look similar to other styles of karate, such as Shōtōkan. Most of the underlying principles, however, were derived from Shindō Yōshin-ryū, an atemi waza focused style of JuJitsu. A block in Wadō may look much like a block in Shōtōkan, but they are executed from different perspectives.

A key principle in Wadō-ryū is that of *Tai sabaki* (often incorrectly referred to as 'evasion'). The Japanese term can be translated as "body-management," and refers to body manipulation so as to move the defender as well as the attacker out of harm's way. The way to achieve this is to 'move along the side rather than to 'move against'—or harmonizewith an aggressor rather than use physical strength to overthrow an opponent. Modern karate competition tends to transform Wadō-ryū away from its roots of this tradition towards a new generic karate that appeals more to the demands of both spectators and competitors.

The founder of Wadō-ryū, Hironori Ōtsuka, was born on 1 June 1892 in Shimodate, Ibaraki Prefecture, Japan. In 1898, Ōtsuka began practicing *koryū jujutsu* under Chojiro Ebashi. From 1905–1921, he studied Shindō Yōshin-ryū jujutsu under Tatsusaburo Nakayama. In 1922, he met Gichin Funakoshi and began to train under him. In 1924, Ōtsuka became one of the first students promoted to black belt in karate by Funakoshi. To broaden his knowledge of Karate, Ōtsuka also studied with other prominent masters such as Kenwa Mabuni of Shitō-ryū and Motobu Chōki. In 1929, Ōtsuka organized the first open school karate club at Tokyo University. Eiichi Eriguchi coined the term 'Wadō-ryū' in 1934.

History of Japanese Martial Arts
Written by Allen Woodman

In 1938, Ōtsuka registered his style of karate with the Dai Nippon Butoku Kai under the name of "Shinshu Wadoryu Karate-Jujutsu." Soon after, however, this was shortened to "Wadō-ryū". In 1938, the Dai Nippon Butoku Kai awarded Ōtsuka the rank of *Renshi-Go*, followed in 1942 by the rank of *Kyoshi-Go*. It was around this time that Tatsuo Suzuki, founder of the WIKF, began training in Wadō-ryū. In 1944, Ōtsuka was appointed Japan's Chief Karate Instructor] In 1946, Ōtsuka awarded Tatsuo Suzuki the rank of 2nd *dan*.The second level black belt.

Around 1950, Jiro Ōtsuka (the founder's second son) began training in Wadō-ryū while in his adolescent years. In 1951, Ōtsuka awarded Suzuki the rank of 5th *dan*, the highest rank awarded in Wadō-ryū at that time. In 1952, the Wadō-ryū headquarters (*honbu*) was established at the Meiji University dojo in Tokyo. In 1954, its name was changed to *Zen Nippon Karate Renmei* (All Japan Karate Federation). In 1955, Ōtsuka published "Karatejutsu no Kenkyu," a book expounding his style of karate. In 1963, he dispatched Suzuki, along with Toru Arakawa and Hajimu

Takashima, to spread Wadō-ryū around the world.

In 1964, the Japan Karate-dō Federation (JKF) was established as a general organization for all karate styles. Wadō-ryū joined this organization as a major group. In 1965, Ōtsuka and Yoshiaki Ajari recorded onto film (which is now still available on two video tapes and DVD) much of the legacy of Wado-Ryu karate. In 1966, Ōtsuka was awarded Kun Goto Soukuo Kyokujujutsu (comparable to a knighthood) by Emperor Hirohito for his dedication to the introduction and teaching of karate. On 5 June 1967, the Wado-Ryu organization changed its name to "Wadōkai."

In 1972, the President of Kokusai Budō Renmei, a member of the Japanese royal family, awarded Ōtsuka the title of *Meijin*. In 1975, Suzuki received his 8th *dan*, the highest grade ever given (at the time) by the Federation of All Japan Karate-dō Organizations, and was named *Hanshi-Go* by the uncle of Emperor Higashikuni.

History of Japanese Martial Arts
Written by Allen Woodman

In 1980, as the result of a conflict between Ōtsuka and the Wadōkai organization, he stepped down as head of the Wadōkai. Eiichi Eriguchi took over his place within that organization. On 1 April 1981, Ōtsuka founded the "Wadōryū Karatedō Renmei." (*Renmei* means "group" or "federation.") After only a few months, he retired as head of this organization. His son, Jiro Ōtsuka,

On 29 January 1982, Hironori Ōtsuka passed away, and in 1983, Jiro Ōtsuka succeeded him as grandmaster of Wadō-ryū. The younger Ōtsuka changed his name to "Hironori Otsuka II" in honor of his late father. In 1989, Tatsuo Suzuki founded the third major Wadō-ryū organization, "Wadō Kokusai" (Wadō International Karatedō Federation; WIKF). (*Kokusai* means "international.") Wadō-ryū outside Japan

Wadō-ryū has been spread to many countries in the world, by both Japanese and non-Japanese students of Hironori Otsuka. Japanese Wadō-ryū

History of Japanese Martial Arts
Written by Allen Woodman

Karate stylists Tatsuo Suzuki, Teruo Kono, Masafumi Shiomitsu, H. Takashima, Naoki Ishikawa, Yoshio Iwasaki and many others spread the art in Europe. Yoshiaki Ajari and Masaru Shintani spread the art in the USA and Canada. Also, non-Japanese such as C.A. Taman (from Indonesia, also the founder of Goshin-Budō Jujutsu Indonesia), Joaquim Gonçalves (from Portugal) and many others has helped to spread the style in their respective countries.Shihan Otto Johnson later began the American Wado-Ryu Renmei in San Bernardino, California.

Ohtsuka Meijin continued to lead the World of Wado-Ryu Karate until the 20th November 1981, when he finally decided to abdicate his possession as Grand Master of Wado-Ryu Karate and nominated his son Hironori Ohtsuka 2nd as his successor. Hironori Ohtsuka Meijin peacefully passed away on 19th January 1982, two months later. Throughout the entire world where Marital Arts are practiced he will always be remembered for his enormous contribution and individual devotion to Wado Karate.

History of Japanese Martial Arts
Written by Allen Woodman

Sensei Hinori Otsuka founder of Wado Ryu
1892-1983

CHAPTER 9

RANKING AND KYU SYSTEM

Throughout the course of karatedo training, it is often taken for granted the grading system that awards belt ranking and titles. Sometimes this system is manifestly personal, with the headmaster--and only he bestowing each promotion directly, according to his own standards. Often, the testing for and awarding of rank is a more bureaucratic affair, with a committee exercising a perfunctory duty in a formally standardized and even routine mannerless ceremony, yet somehow more officious.

History of Japanese Martial Arts
Written by Allen Woodman

The writings of Hanshi Richard Kim of the Butoku-kai (Dojo Fall 1993) taught how the dan/kyu (degree) system was adopted by modern budo systems, promulgated by the Butoku-kai, and codified in its final form for Japanese karatedo by the Federation of All Japan Karatedo Organizations (FAJKO). To truly understand this ranking system, it is important to gain a clearer insight into how the various masters obtained their ranking, since that forms the basis for your rank.

This much we know for certain: On April 12, 1924, Gichin Funakoshi, the "Father of Modern Karate," awarded karate's first black belt dan upon seven men. The recipients included Hironori Ohtsuka, founder of wado-ryu karatedo, Shinken Gima, later of gima-ha shoto-ryu, and Ante Tokuda, Gima's cousin, who received a nidan (second degree) black belt. Like Gima, Tokuda had trained extensively in Okinawa before coming to Japan proper. The others were Kasuya, Akiba, Shimizu and Hirose. This beginning was a highly personal, yet formal ceremony in which Funakoshi is said to have handed out lengths of black belting to his pupils. Still there is no evidence that Funakoshi himself had ranking in any budo under the dan/kyu system.

Actually, Funakoshi was greatly influenced by Jigoro Kano, aristocratic founder of judo, and originator of the dan/kyu system. Kano was a highly respected individual, and Funakoshi prided himself on being an educated and "proper" man who rightly believed that he was acting correctly. Kano's system was not only being applied to judo, but to other budo as well under the aegis of the Butoku-kai and the Japanese Ministry of Education. Funakoshi, then, just adopted the order of the day: a ranking system officially sanctioned by Japan's greatest martial arts entities. Funakoshi's own rank was of no consequence, since it seems that belt ranking was really just something for the students, not for headmasters.

For its part, the Butoku-kai issued instructor's licenses: the titles renshi (the lowest), kyoshi, and hanshi (the highest). It would be a while before the dan/kyu system became universal in karate. By the end of the 1930s, each karate group was called upon to register with the butoku-kai for official sanctioning, and in 1938, a meeting of the Butoku-kai's official karatedo leaders was held in Tokyo. Its purpose was to discuss the standards for awarding rank within their art. Attending, among others, were,

Photographed at a meeting to amlgemate ranking credentials for martialArts
Gichin Funakoshi, Chojun Miyagi, Hironori Ohtsuka, Kenwa Mabuni, Kensei Kinjo, Sannosuke Ueshima, Tatsuo Yamada, and Gogen Yamaguchi

Hironori Ohtsuka of wado-ryu, Kenwa Mabuni of shito-ryu Kensei Kinjo (Kaneshiro) and Sannosuke Ueshima of kushin-ryu, Tatsuo Yamada of Nippon kempo, Koyu Konishi of shindo-jinen-ryu, and a young Gogen Yamaguchi of goju-ryu.

Most of these men were founders of their own styles, and as such automatically became the highest rank that their agreed-on respective standards allowed. Yamaguchi assumed leadership of goju-ryu because, we are told, goju-ryu's founder, Chojun Miyagi, personally asked him to take the leadership of the style in Japan. Around the same time Funakoshi had finalized the grading standards for use at his shotokan dojo. Of course, the Butoku-kai continued to sanction head teachers directly. This was not without controversy, however, since Konishi sat on the board that awarded Funakoshi his renshi and Konishi had been Funakoshi's student. Of course, Konishi had inside ties to the Butoku-kai by virtue of birth, something the Okinawan Funakoshi could not have.

Back on Okinawa, the dan/kyu system did not become universal until after World War II. It was not unknown there, however, and some individual teachers did utilize the black belt. Judo had been practiced on

History of Japanese Martial Arts
Written by Allen Woodman

Okinawa at least since the 1920s. In fact, it was at a Judo Black Belt Association (Yudanshakai) meeting on Okinawa that Miyagi and shito-ryu's Kenwa Mabuni demonstrated karate kata (forms) for Jigoro Kano garnering praises from the judo founder. Miyagi, it should be noted, became the first karate expert given the title of kyoshi (master) from the butoku-kai in 1937. Miyagi was then appointed chief of its Okinawan branch

After the ravages of war in the Pacific, the surviving karate leaders had to begin anew. With the Butoku-kai administration shut down for years to come, each karate group was on its own. The acknowledged leaders of each faction, as well as individual dojo chiefs, gave out dan ranks based upon all original sanctioning by the Butoku-kai or mandates inherited directly from the ryu's founder.

Rushing in to fill the vacuum left by the Butoku-kai, various dojo coalesced to perpetuate the art and legitimize its members' ranks. In the late 1940s and early 1950s, each new association, including the Gojukai, Shito-kai, Chito-kai, Shotokai and Japan Karate associations codified their rules and issued rank accordingly. Generally, several instructors created a board of directors or council to govern the association. Some officer, be it the chief instructor, president, director or chairman would have signature authority on menjo (rank certificates). In this way, the senior-most members would attain their rank by being acknowledged and "signed off" by the board or committee. Other times, a senior member of one faction would attain high enough rank from the faction-head to then go out and form his own style or organization. Supposedly, the famous Masutatsu Oyama received his eighth dan from Goju-kai head Gogen Yamaguchi. Oyama later formed his own style that was not completely a type of goju-ryu.

Usually in a legalistic and officious way these groups would simply adopt or adhere to some even higher authority or granting agency to further legitimize their actions. Recognition by the Japanese Ministry of Education was the ultimate sanction for individuals and groups in these times. Also new associations -- both in Japan proper and in Okinawa --

appeared. These became the grantor ranking authority, much in the way the Butoku-kai had acted previously. These new organizations were to set the pattern and be the original source for today's ranking. As with the single-style clubs, the head instructors often assumed the rank for which they were qualified, based on criteria they wrote themselves.

One of the first was the All Japan Karatedo Federation, which seems to have started shortly after World War II as a confederation of headmasters such as Funakoshi, Chitose, Mabuni, Yamaguchi and Toyama. They regularized the dan/kyu system to some extent, and with this group the modern Japanese karate ranking system became the norm. This unity did not last however. For example, the ranking was not consistent from group to group in the upper levels. The shotokan associations such as the JKA and the Shotokai only used up to godan (fifth rank) at this time. As a result, some groups had ceased to participate by the early 1950s.

History of Japanese Martial Arts
Written by Allen Woodman

Even more reminiscent of the Butokukai was the International Martial Arts Federation (IMAF), known as the Kokusai Budoin. Originally named the National Japan Health Association, IMAF was launched in 1952 by powerful martial artists from several disciplines. From judo there was Kyuzo Mifune, Kazuo Ito and Shizuo Sato. From kendo came Hakudo Nakayama and Hiromasa Takano, and from karatedo there was Hironori Ohtsuka. Its first chairman was Prince Tsunenori Kaya. From the start, IMAF was set up by senior martial artists to preserve and promote various budo to create a mutually supportive network. A ranking system consisting of first through tenth dan, as well as the title system of renshi, kyoshi and hanshi, was adopted. Now highly respected and skilled instructors could have a direct avenue for promotion themselves. Several karateka including Gogen Yamaguchi, Hironori Ohtsuka (I and II), and more recently, Hirokazu Kanazawa of shotokan, received their highest grades through IMAF.

For Okinawa, the dan/kyu system did not really take hold until 1956, with the formation of the Okinawa Karate Association (OKF). Chosin Chibana, first to name his system shorin-ryu, was the first president. According to the historical data of the Shudokan (a Japanese group started by Kanken Toyama in Tokyo), Chibana and Toyama were officially recognized by the Japanese Ministry of Education to grant any rank in the art of karate, regardless of style. Chibana helped organize the OKF, and it was then that the mainstream Okinawan groups, on a widespread basis, began differentiating their black belt ranks as other than simple teacher and student demarcations.

A talented and, some say, colorful character, Toyama gave several certifications as a largess to dojo heads in Okinawa and Japan proper. These were usually shibucho ("superintendent," from the feudal area commander title) diplomas. These certifications set up the individuals so named as head of their own branch of the All Japan Karatedo Federation and, by extension, of their own groups. Eizo Shimabuku, founder of the shobayashi-ryu/shorin-ryu faction, traces his own tenth dan to a Toyama certification.

Shimabuku's assumption of the tenth dan, and his wearing of a red belt, was not without dispute, and it was controversies of this type that led most Okinawan leaders to eschew the red belt altogether.

The AJKF did not last as a unified group of different styles in Japan proper. Toyama's foray back to Okinawa did lead later to the formation of the AJKF-Okinawa Branch with the organizing help of Isamu Tamotsu. Tamotsu became a student of Okinawa's Zenryo Shimabuku (of Kyan-type shorinryu) and would become known as the soke (style head) of the Japanese faction of Shorinji-ryu. In 1960, the Okinawan branch of the AJKF organized with Zenryo Shimabuku as president. A constituent group of this AJKF was the Okinawa Kempo League headed up by Shigeru Nakamura and Zenryo Shimabuku as a loose confederation of various technique sharing dojo.

Like other associations, the AJKF Okinawa Branch provided for the ranking of its member instructors. It operated as a rival to the Okinawa Karate Federation. However, it did not last long either and its member schools drifted away and formed other alliances. Its emblem did not die, however. The same patch is still used by Tsuyoshi Chitose's Chito-kai.

The central karate leaders continued on their own or became part of other groups, using authority inherited mostly from members of one of the original Okinawan organizations, the most significant is the All Okinawa Karate and Kobudo Rengokai. Formed by Seitoku Higa as a successor to the Okinawa Federation in 1967, the Okinawa detail of the emblem was used to distinguish each member group. Seiyu Oyata can be seen wearing this patch in Dojo, fall 1993, page 13.

Chitose was a founding member of the original Japanese AJKF, but his tenth dan was issued in 1958, according to the Chitokai, by the All Okinawa Karate Kobudo Rengokai. His hanshi title was issued by the same group in 1962. This is confusing however, since the AOKK-Rengokai was not formed until 1967. It grew out of an earlier group: the Okinawa Kobudo Federation that was organized in 1961.

This later group was organized by Seitoku Higa (of various lineages related to shorin-ryu) and Seikichi Uehara (molobu-ryu). Higa had been ranked by Toyama while living in Japan and may have been connected with the original AJKF.

The most significant event in the use of the dan/kyu system in karate was the formation of the FAJKO in 1964. All the major groups and factions of Japanese karatedo were brought under FAJKO's umbrella. By 1971, a ranking structure was adopted that standardized all the systems. High rank was issued to FAJKO member instructors by the organization's board. In this way, heads of constituent organizations could be upgraded, much as in earlier attempts at confederacy. An earlier, but smaller, confederacy of schools with rank-sanctioning authority was the Japan Karatedo Rengokai, which still exists and is a member of FAJKO.

After the birth of FAJKO, the JKA upgraded its own ranking requirements to conform. Sixth and eighth dans were awarded in the JKA back in the mid-1960s, and

Hidetaka Nishiyama in Los Angeles was one of those upgraded at that time. Though not all groups participate in FAJKO these days, most still are tied to that organization in terms of rank structure and sanction. Others, not so tied, have conformed to the FAJKO criteria and standards nonetheless.

Shortly after FAJKO was launched, the Okinawans formed the All Okinawa Karatedo Federation as a successor to the old OKF. Members of both the OKF and AJKF-Okinawa Branch became part of the new association. Some of Okinawa's most mainstream karate leaders formed the AOKF board. These included Nagamine, Zenryo Shimabuku, Meitoku Yagi of gojuryu, Kanei Uechi of uechi-ryu and Yuchoku Higa of shorin-ryu. They adopted a dan/kyu and renshi, kyoshi, hanshi (plus a hanshisei) system almost identical to FAJKOs.

Other karate leaders continued on their own or became part of other groups, using authority inherited mostly from members of one of the original Okinawan organizations. The most significant is the All Okinawa Karate and Kobudo Rengokai. Formed by Seitku Higa as a successor to the Okinawa Kobudo Federation in 1967, the Okinawa Rengokai also adopted very similar standards to the AOKF. Higa's organizations had certified as hanshi--and hence supreme instructor--several who were style or group heads in their own right. These included Shinsuke Kaneshima of Tozan-ryu from shurite, Hohan Soken of matsumura shorin-ryu, Shinpo Matayoshi of matayoshi kobudo Kenko Nakaima of ryuel-ryu, ShianToma of shorin-ryu (Kyan type) and motobu-ryu, Tatsuo Shimabuku of isshin-ryu, Shosei Kina of uhuchiku kobudo, and Zenryo Shimabuku of shorin-ryu.

It is clear that karate ranks sprang from several original sources. It was a relatively modem construct on an old martial art ideal. It was issued by individuals and institutions with set standards that were recognized by other prestigious groups and individuals. And this is the crux of the matter: For rank to be recognized, the bestower must be recognized within karate's mainstream community. It must be based in tradition, and linked to a body or sanctioned individual who is perceived as beyond reproach. The standards by which rank is achieved and given must be recognizable, and conform to already existing norms in the Okinawan/Japanese martial arts hierarchy. Anyone can print up or write a fancy certificate, but absent of any governmental or legal guidelines, it is the recognition and acceptance by existing groups and institutions that give each ranking group or individual its legitimacy.

The development of the ranking system is a typically human development, with rivalries and contradictions, and our own masters received their rank in different ways. The highest-ranked of the old masters did not- could not-receive the tenth dan from their "style." They were invariably ranked by someone else and applied this grade to their own group. This is still true. As in a medieval European knighting, originally any knight could dub another, then regal institutions took over. However, it is the skill and knowledge that gains the rank, not vice versa.

The quest for rank, misses the point.

CHAPTER 10

LOOKING FOR OURSELVES

"First know yourself, and then know others."
Gichin Funakoshi, founder of karate

After many years of research and study and with the advent of the internet and mass media the true history of Budo can be definitive. The clarity of the roots and its strong foundations only keep the arts in question true to their own traditions and to the founding fathers ideologies of the arts they created.

History of Japanese Martial Arts
Written by Allen Woodman

When we look back as humans in the time slip of evolution this may seem a trite and insignificant matter to discuss. However, learning where we all have come from, the people and places that our great ancestors derived their lives and the culture from, only strengthen our resolve to keep their faiths alive and protected. With these ideals in mind I sat down to write these stories of what I believe to be true masters as well as the patriarchs of our societies today. These few brave men and women from our past directed such an understanding and complete form of expression that would ultimately continue through not only hundreds of years but yet to be seen thousands of years to come.

The future is yet to be written, yet it is with these few people that our destiny has been entrenched and secured. The unknown countless hours and years of dedication and commitment that each person devoted to his or her style is what we as martial artist strive to recreate in their image.

These few are not gods; they were not politicians nor were they business men or women. They only believed in the martial art they taught to each and every student. They would become our masters and teachers. They are the founders of thousands of new systems and additional art forms that have arisen since their inception of each art respectively.

Martial artist are rarely good businessmen. The sense of making and earning or a living was never a conscious thought of their pursuit of perfection in themselves or their arts. I feel it should never be either. The Martial arts are just that, an art form like any other art form, like that of painting or dancing or writing. These libertarians did more than create a self defense system that could dismay and disarm an opponent. These arts were the gift left to us as humans inhabiting the same earthly soil. We as humans all inherently share the same goal of self betterment through one's own actions and abilities. These abilities take time to master and even more resolve to understand in full. But that was the legacy of each art. To find your own path to a richer and better understanding of ourselves in the footsteps of those who walked before us and showed us a path to follow.

It has never been a rule to do as they have done but rather understanding the rules they put forth to do what we must, continue on in their endeavors and in their spirit. We must be true Martial Artist. Even more importantly true to ourselves.

Understanding where we came from as the direction to know where we may ultimately go.

SIDEKICK PUBLICATIONS
WWW.SIDEKICKPUBLICATION.COM (619) 851-5672 / (702) 773-2786

My Karate a personal journey: a personal journey
Authored by Mr. Allen Woodman

List Price: **$14.99** 6" x 9" (15.24 x 22.86 cm)
Black & White on White paper
182 pages

ISBN-13: 978-1456351298
ISBN-10: 145635129X
BISAC: Sports & Recreation / Martial Arts & Self-Defense

This is one man's journey to find the true path in martial arts. Sensei Allen Woodman, brings you in to the private world of sacred and often secret world of traditional martial arts training. With personal anecdotes and other humorous stories he gives you the reader an insider's look at training with some of the world's greatest Master and top instructors.

Taizan Ryu Taiho Jutsu: Military and civilian police tactics
Authored by Joseph Miller, Authored by Mr. Allen Woodman

List Price: **$14.99**

6" x 9" (15.24 x 22.86 cm)
Black & White on White paper
90 pages

ISBN-13: 978-1460913154
ISBN-10: 1460913159
BISAC: Sports & Recreation / Martial Arts & Self-Defense

Taizan Ryu Taiho Jutsu founded by Soke Joe Miller, a 50 year veteran of martial arts, 8th degree black belt and the leading authority and founder of Taizan Ryu Taiho Jutsu system. This complete manual has all 18 techniques that have been patented by the U.S. Government to train both Civilians and military.

Sandokan: The Cutting Edge Martial Art
Authored by Mr. Les Kiersnowski

List Price: **$24.95**

7" x 10" (17.78 x 25.4 cm)
Black & White bleed on White paper
152 pages

ISBN-13: 978-1491092187
ISBN-10: 1491092181
BISAC: Sports & Recreation / Martial Arts & Self-Defense

The Sandokan system is based on physics, principals of martial science and the science of anatomy. Achieving this martial arts system has encompassed many years of traditional and practical development. It is a system based on the perfecting of body positioning for maximum output of energy.

The Healing Touch Student Workbook: Taizan Ryu Student Workbook
Authored by Mr. Renshi Allen Woodman / Soke Joe Miller

List Price: **$29.95**

8.5" x 11" (21.59 x 27.94 cm)
Black & White on White paper
104 pages

ISBN-13: 978-1468182668
ISBN-10: 1468182668
BISAC: Health & Fitness / Acupressure & Acupuncture

This is the full student workbook designed to instruct each person to full certification in the art of Japanese Shiatsu massage and finger point pressure techniques.

The Healing Touch: Shiatsu and massage
Authored by Soke Joe Miller / Mr. Allen Woodman

List Price: **$39.95**

8.5" x 11" (21.59 x 27.94 cm)
Black & White on White paper
202 pages

ISBN-13: 978-1468139136
ISBN-10: 1468139134
BISAC: Medical / Healing

The Healing Touch of Japanese Shiatsu brought to you in a informative and insightful way. Taught by a leading authority in traditional Japanese acupuncture.

The Martial Directory 2012
Authored by Allen Woodman

List Price: **$45.00** / List Price: **$99.00**

8.5" x 11" (21.59 x 27.94 cm)
Black & White on White paper / Full Color Version
324 pages

ISBN-13: 978-1479198542 - B/W
ISBN-13: 978-1479200527 - Full Color
BISAC: Biography & Autobiography / Sports

North American Who's Who in martial arts. The best of the best for 2012. Learn the history and biographies of the masters and instructors that shape the world of martial arts in America today. Legends like Cynthia Rothrock, Eric Lee, Jason Lau and many more. Great Masters past and present share stories of success and training in the world of martial arts.

The Martial Directory 2014: International Martial Arts Guide
Authored by Mr. Allen Woodman

List Price: **$65.00** / **$129.00** Full Color

8.5" x 11" (21.59 x 27.94 cm)
Black & White Bleed on White paper
310 pages

ISBN-13: 978-1494480134 B/W
ISBN-13: 978-1494480301 Full Color
BISAC: Biography & Autobiography / Sports

International Who's Who in martial arts. The best of the best for 2014. Learn the history and biographies of the masters and instructors that shape the world of martial arts in America today. Read the true history of some of the greatest martial a foot of all time. Masters and instructors from every martial art imaginable.

The Samurai Way: Bushido Origins of Modern day martial arts
Authored by Mr. Grant A. Miller, Cover design or artwork by Mr. Allen Woodman, Cover design or artwork by Mr. Allen Woodman

List Price: **$14.95**

6" x 9" (15.24 x 22.86 cm)
Black & White bleed on White paper
130 pages

ISBN-13: 978-1484086478
ISBN-10: 1484086473
BISAC: Sports & Recreation / Martial Arts & Self-Defense

This book explores the revelation of AikiJujutsu that was discovered through the accumulation of hundreds of years of training and study. An all-encompassing philosophy that can be found in nearly every major Asian martial arts discipline.

Traditional Martial Arts Philosophy: For the Mind, Body and Spirit
Authored by Mr. Tom Thurston, Authored by Mr. Chang Kiwan Choi

List Price: **$19.95**

6" x 9" (15.24 x 22.86 cm)
Black & White on White paper
248 pages

ISBN-13: 978-1481980333
ISBN-10: 1481980335
BISAC: Health & Fitness / Reference

Drawing from their many decades of experience as traditional martial arts practitioners, competitors, teachers, demonstrators and advocates, Grand Master C.K. Choi and Master Tom Thurston eloquently and effectively present of what it means to be a dedicated traditional martial artist.

Universal Warrior Arts System: Spiritually Motivating Inspiration for Self Defense
Authored by Austin Wright Sr.,

List Price: **$19.95**

7" x 10" (17.78 x 25.4 cm)
Black & White bleed on White paper
182 pages

ISBN-13: 978-1492742043
ISBN-10: 149274204X
BISAC: Sports & Recreation / Martial Arts & Self-Defense

Universal Warrior Arts is an Empowering Self-Defense and Life Skill Strategy Guide book for the Mind, Body and Spiritual Warfare The goal and objective of this book is to incorporate your own vertical Ju-Jitsu Skills, Violence Prevention, Spiritual Inspiration, Intervention, and Street Survival Awareness Tactics for Family Safety purposes.

Wushu Skills
Authored by Kenny Perez

List Price: **$26.95**

7" x 10" (17.78 x 25.4 cm)
Black & White on White paper
258 pages

ISBN-13: 978-1492734734
ISBN-10: 149273473X
BISAC: Sports & Recreation / Martial Arts & Self-Defense

Master Perez has competed in major martial arts tournaments since the 70s. He was a three-time member of the U.S. Wushu team. His skills have given him opportunities to work in the movie industry as an actor, stuntman and fight choreographer. He has worked with legendary director Yuen Wo Ping, Donnie Yen and Jet Li. Wushu Skills is the complete book on the ancient art.

JEET KUNE DO: THE SYSTEM WITHOUT A SYSTEM
Authored by George Hainesr

List Price: **$39.95**

8.3 x 11 inches

Black and White 488 Pages

ISBN-10: 1420832158
ISBN-13: 978-1420832150

Step by step instructions to help you develop a deeper understanding of the art of Jeet Kune Do. This book consists of over 3300 photos of in-depth instructions, based on the Original Jeet Kune Do. This book is a must for every serious Martial Artist of any style. The Instructions in this book will help you develop a better and deeper understanding of Jeet Kune Do and scientific street self-defense.

SIDEKICK PUBLICATIONS
WWW.SIDEKICKPUBLICATION.COM (619) 851-5672 / (702) 773-2786

Bushido The Soul Of Japan: The Soul Of Japan
Authored by Mr. Inazo Nitobe PHD, Editorial coordination by Allen Woodman
List Price: **$18.95**

6" x 9" (15.24 x 22.86 cm)
Black & White on White paper
76 pages

ISBN-13: 978-1477626436
ISBN-10: 1477626433
BISAC: Education / Professional Development

The Code of the warrior. This traditional Japanese text as written by Dr. Inazo Nitobe in 1904 edited and published by Allen Woodman. This is a detailed understanding of the traditional Samurai Code of life.

Fundamental Karate B/W: Taikyoku Shodan - Heian Sandan
Authored by Allen Woodman
List Price: **$29.95**

8.5" x 8.5" (21.59 x 21.59 cm)
Black & White on White paper
194 pages

ISBN-13: 978-1475126242
ISBN-10: 1475126247
BISAC: Sports & Recreation / Martial Arts & Self-Defense

Fundamental Karate is the first in a series of books written by Renshi Sensei Allen Woodman on the traditional art of Shotokan Karate Do. Trained in Japan for over 25 years, Sensei Allen brings the art of Japan to the U.S.A.

History of Japanese Martial Arts
Authored by Mr. Allen Woodman
List Price: **$18.99**

5.5" x 8.5" (13.97 x 21.59 cm)
Black & White on White paper
70 pages

ISBN-13: 978-1460956540
ISBN-10: 1460956547
BISAC: Sports & Recreation / Martial Arts & Self-Defense

History of Japanese Martial Arts is the first in a series of frank and well researched informational book about the true origins of all the major forms of traditional Japanese Martial Arts. Learn the true history of BUDO and its founding fathers.

Hojojutsu: The art of tying your enemy
Authored by Mr. Shihan Allen Woodman, Photographs by Mr. Brian Smith
List Price: **$24.95**

7" x 10" (17.78 x 25.4 cm)
Black & White Bleed on White paper
132 pages

ISBN-13: 978-1482755657
ISBN-10: 1482755653
BISAC: Sports & Recreation / Martial Arts & Self-Defense

Hojojutsu is the traditional Japanese martial art of restraining a person using cord or rope. Encompassing many different materials, techniques and methods from many different schools, this is one of the only books ever published on this art form detailing the defensive practices and techniques of the art.

Introduction to American Wado Ryu:
Authored by Allen Woodman, Authored by Dr. Otto Johnson
List Price: **$19.95**

7" x 10" (17.78 x 25.4 cm)
Black & White on White paper
56 pages

ISBN-13: 978-1475125313
ISBN-10: 1475125313
BISAC: Sports & Recreation / Martial Arts & Self-Defense

Introduction to American Wado Ryu By the late Hanshi Otto Johnson and Renshi Allen Woodman. This is the last and only publication for the authentic art of Wado R= as per the requirements of the American Wado Ryu Federation International and the American Wado Ryu Association.

Komugi's Dream
Authored by Mrs. Taeko Tawada, & Mr. Allen Woodman, Illustrated by Mrs Yuka Sasaki
List Price: **$9.95**

8.5" x 8.5" (21.59 x 21.59 cm)
Full Color on White paper
40 pages

ISBN-13: 978-1481811101
ISBN-10: 148181110X
BISAC: Education / Collaborative & Team Teaching

Komugi's Dream is a special children's book designed for young readers. Written in both Japanese and English this book serves as a platform book to help young Bilingual readers understand the story in full style with beautifully illustrated Full Color pictures. Each page reads in both traditional Japanese and English text.

Korean Samurai An American Dream
Authored by Dr Sung Woo Kahm, Authored by Jayne VanHise Bruinooge
List Price: **$19.95**

7" x 10" (17.78 x 25.4 cm)
Black & White on White paper
140 pages

ISBN-13: 978-1481968409
ISBN-10: 1481968408
BISAC: Biography & Autobiography / Personal Memoirs

Korean Samurai An American dream is a true story that reflects the life and success of Grandmaster Kahm Sung Woo from early childhood in Korea to a new life in the United States of America. From his turbulent times and that ran the military and service to a fashion to the world of motion pictures and building an empire in the world of martial arts.

Man By Choice Male by Birth: Male Metamorphic Interruptus
Authored by Dr. Michael Willett
List Price: **$19.95**

6" x 9" (15.24 x 22.86 cm)
Black & White on White paper
222 pages

ISBN-13: 978-1492705420
ISBN-10: 149270542X
BISAC: Family & Relationships / Interpersonal Relations

Affectionately dubbed, the "Warrior Priest" by New York's News 1's Roma Torre, Dr. Willett one of the world's renowned martial arts instructors. In the amazing pages you are going to hear deep introspection of males that became men by way of their great trials, missteps, blunders and just bonehead decisions.

Martial Arts Guide to Success: Karate International
Authored by Mr. Michael DePasquale Jr., Authored by Mr. Allen Woodman
List Price: **$49.95**

8.5" x 11" (21.59 x 27.94 cm)
Black & White on White paper
326 pages

ISBN-13: 978-1458160086
ISBN-10: 1458160087
BISAC: Business & Economics / Advertising & Promotion

Both Michael DePasquale Jr. and Renshi Allen Woodman bring you a true perspective and practical business advice to open run and effectively manage a martial arts school.

Monkey Kung Fu: History and Tradition
Authored by Mr Michael Matsuda, Prepared for publication by Mr. Allen Woodman
List Price: **$29.95**

7.5" x 9.25" (19.05 x 23.495 cm)
Black & White on White paper
218 pages

ISBN-13: 978-1492232681
ISBN-10: 1492232688
BISAC: Sports & Recreation / Martial Arts & Self-Defense

Monkey Style Kung Fu It is perhaps, the rarest and most secretive style of Chinese kung fu. There is only one Monkey kung fu style when in fact, there are three. One of them is thousands of years old and another is only a mere 100 years old. They include.

Museum Honor Awards: Martial Arts History Museum
Authored by Mr. Michael Matsuda, Prepared for publication by Mr. Allen Woodman
List Price: **$22.95**

8.25" x 8.25" (20.955 x 20.955 cm)
Black & White on White paper
186 pages

ISBN-13: 978-1492213277
ISBN-10: 1492213276
BISAC: Sports & Recreation / Martial Arts & Self-Defense

From the inspiration, planning and coordinating by the museum board members Michael Matsuda, Art Camacho, Rafael Kosche, Fariborz Azhakh and J.D. Bowles, the coveted Museum Honor Awards ceremony was officially launched. The Museum

The Martial Arts History Museum: How it all began
Authored by Mr. Michael Matsuda, Prepared for publication by Mr. Allen Woodman
List Price: **$29.95**

7.44" x 9.69" (18.898 x 24.613 cm)
Black & White on White paper
314 pages

ISBN-13: 978-1492213697
ISBN-10: 1492213691
BISAC: History / Historiography

This book is the story of how it all began with the historic opening of The Martial Arts History Museum.

MASTERING WING CHUN
Authored by Tony Massengill / Samuel Kwok

$29.95 Per Copy

7 x 10.1 inches
297 pages

ISBN-10: 1933901268
ISBN-13: 978-1933901268

In this book, the keys to the Ip Man Wing Chun Kung Fu system are explained. The three hand sets are shown in detail, along with the application of the key movements.

KEYS TO WING CHUN
Authored by Samuel Kwok

$44.95 Per Copy

7.9 x 7.9 inches
171 pages

ISBN-10: 9789671133804

This is an essential tool for anyone looking to improve all their skill and learn to master the martial art Wing Chun! Those of you looking for a definitive guide to Wing Chun or a back-up to your own study and practice will not be disappointed by this book. It covers everything about the hand forms and some history and philosophy about Wing Chun in General.

MASTERING ESKRIMA DISARMS
Authored by Mark V Wiley

$39.95 Per Copy

10 x 7 x 0.5 inches
254 pages

ISBN-10: 1481160646
ISBN-13: 978-1481160643

In this comprehensive book you will learn the disarming techniques of over 30 different styles of Eskrima, Kali, Arnis and Kaberoan, including their essential principles

THE BASIC SURVIVAL GUIDE TO THE ZOMBIE APOCOLYPSE
Authored By Allen Woodman

$19.95 Per Copy

ISBN-10:
ISBN-13:

This book contains effective survival techniques for any natural disaster, including basic survival skills to learn how to build a shelter, purify water, and open a tin can without a can opener or tool. Learn where to go during a disaster and where not to go. What tools will you need if the Zombie apocalypse comes?

For More information on Shihan Allen Woodman Please contact at senseiallenwoodman@yahoo.com

Or view his website at www.senseiallenwoodman.com

Printed in Great Britain
by Amazon